DENG XIAOPING

WORLD LEADERS   PAST & PRESENT

DENG XIAOPING

Wendy Lubetkin

YB
Deng Xiaoping

CHELSEA HOUSE PUBLISHERS
NEW YORK
NEW HAVEN   PHILADELPHIA

EDITOR-IN-CHIEF: Nancy Toff
EXECUTIVE EDITOR: Remmel T. Nunn
MANAGING EDITOR: Karyn Gullen Browne
COPY CHIEF: Juliann Barbato
PICTURE EDITOR: Adrian G. Allen
ART DIRECTOR: Giannella Garrett
MANUFACTURING MANAGER: Gerald Levine

Staff for DENG XIAOPING:

SENIOR EDITOR: John W. Selfridge
ASSISTANT EDITOR: Sean Dolan
COPY EDITOR: Terrance Dolan
EDITORIAL ASSISTANT: Sean Ginty
ASSOCIATE PICTURE EDITOR: Juliette Dickstein
PICTURE RESEARCHER: Toby Greenberg
SENIOR DESIGNER: David Murray
ASSISTANT DESIGNER: Jill Goldreyer
PRODUCTION COORDINATOR: Joseph Romano
COVER ILLUSTRATION: Kye Carbone

CREATIVE DIRECTOR: Harold Steinberg

First Printing

1 3 5 7 9 8 6 4 2

Library of Congress Cataloging in Publication Data

Lubetkin, Wendy.

Deng Xiaoping/Wendy Lubetkin.
p. cm.—(World leaders past & present)
Bibliography: p.
Includes index.
Summary: A biography of the Chinese leader who lost all his offices
during the Chinese Cultural Revolution but later returned to power and
now serves as chairman of the Central Advisory Commission to the
Communist Party.

ISBN 1-55546-830-6
1. Teng, Hsiao-p'ing, 1904– —Juvenile literature.
2. Heads of state—China—Biography—Juvenile literature.
3. China—Politics and government—20th century—Juvenile
literature. [1. Teng, Hsiao-p'ing, 1904– 2. Heads of state.]
I. Title. II. Series.
DS778.T39L83   1988
951.05′8′0924—dc 19
[B]
[92] 87-26582 CIP AC

Contents

JOHN ADAMS
JOHN QUINCY ADAMS
KONRAD ADENAUER
ALEXANDER THE GREAT
SALVADOR ALLENDE
MARC ANTONY
CORAZON AQUINO
YASIR ARAFAT
KING ARTHUR
HAFEZ AL-ASSAD
KEMAL ATATÜRK
ATTILA
CLEMENT ATTLEE
AUGUSTUS CAESAR
MENACHEM BEGIN
DAVID BEN-GURION
OTTO VON BISMARCK
LÉON BLUM
SIMON BOLÍVAR
CESARE BORGIA
WILLY BRANDT
LEONID BREZHNEV
JULIUS CAESAR
JOHN CALVIN
JIMMY CARTER
FIDEL CASTRO
CATHERINE THE GREAT
CHARLEMAGNE
CHIANG KAI-SHEK
WINSTON CHURCHILL
GEORGES CLEMENCEAU
CLEOPATRA
CONSTANTINE THE GREAT
HERNÁN CORTÉS
OLIVER CROMWELL
GEORGES-JACQUES
  DANTON
JEFFERSON DAVIS
MOSHE DAYAN
CHARLES DE GAULLE
EAMON DE VALERA
EUGENE DEBS
DENG XIAOPING
BENJAMIN DISRAELI
ALEXANDER DUBČEK
FRANÇOIS & JEAN-CLAUDE
  DUVALIER
DWIGHT EISENHOWER
ELEANOR OF AQUITAINE
ELIZABETH I
FAISAL
FERDINAND & ISABELLA
FRANCISCO FRANCO
BENJAMIN FRANKLIN

FREDERICK THE GREAT
INDIRA GANDHI
MOHANDAS GANDHI
GIUSEPPE GARIBALDI
AMIN & BASHIR GEMAYEL
GENGHIS KHAN
WILLIAM GLADSTONE
MIKHAIL GORBACHEV
ULYSSES S. GRANT
ERNESTO "CHE" GUEVARA
TENZIN GYATSO
ALEXANDER HAMILTON
DAG HAMMARSKJÖLD
HENRY VIII
HENRY OF NAVARRE
PAUL VON HINDENBURG
HIROHITO
ADOLF HITLER
HO CHI MINH
KING HUSSEIN
IVAN THE TERRIBLE
ANDREW JACKSON
JAMES I
WOJCIECH JARUZELSKI
THOMAS JEFFERSON
JOAN OF ARC
POPE JOHN XXIII
POPE JOHN PAUL II
LYNDON JOHNSON
BENITO JUÁREZ
JOHN KENNEDY
ROBERT KENNEDY
JOMO KENYATTA
AYATOLLAH KHOMEINI
NIKITA KHRUSHCHEV
KIM IL SUNG
MARTIN LUTHER KING, JR.
HENRY KISSINGER
KUBLAI KHAN
LAFAYETTE
ROBERT E. LEE
VLADIMIR LENIN
ABRAHAM LINCOLN
DAVID LLOYD GEORGE
LOUIS XIV
MARTIN LUTHER
JUDAS MACCABEUS
JAMES MADISON
NELSON & WINNIE
  MANDELA
MAO ZEDONG
FERDINAND MARCOS
GEORGE MARSHALL

MARY, QUEEN OF SCOTS
TOMÁŠ MASARYK
GOLDA MEIR
KLEMENS VON METTERNICH
JAMES MONROE
HOSNI MUBARAK
ROBERT MUGABE
BENITO MUSSOLINI
NAPOLÉON BONAPARTE
GAMAL ABDEL NASSER
JAWAHARLAL NEHRU
NERO
NICHOLAS II
RICHARD NIXON
KWAME NKRUMAH
DANIEL ORTEGA
MOHAMMED REZA PAHLAVI
THOMAS PAINE
CHARLES STEWART
  PARNELL
PERICLES
JUAN PERÓN
PETER THE GREAT
POL POT
MUAMMAR EL-QADDAFI
RONALD REAGAN
CARDINAL RICHELIEU
MAXIMILIEN ROBESPIERRE
ELEANOR ROOSEVELT
FRANKLIN ROOSEVELT
THEODORE ROOSEVELT
ANWAR SADAT
HAILE SELASSIE
PRINCE SIHANOUK
JAN SMUTS
JOSEPH STALIN
SUKARNO
SUN YAT-SEN
TAMERLANE
MOTHER TERESA
MARGARET THATCHER
JOSIP BROZ TITO
TOUSSAINT L'OUVERTURE
LEON TROTSKY
PIERRE TRUDEAU
HARRY TRUMAN
QUEEN VICTORIA
LECH WALESA
GEORGE WASHINGTON
CHAIM WEIZMANN
WOODROW WILSON
XERXES
EMILIANO ZAPATA
ZHOU ENLAI

CHELSEA HOUSE PUBLISHERS

ON LEADERSHIP

Arthur M. Schlesinger, jr.

LEADERSHIP, it may be said, is really what makes the world go round. Love no doubt smooths the passage; but love is a private transaction between consenting adults. Leadership is a public transaction with history. The idea of leadership affirms the capacity of individuals to move, inspire, and mobilize masses of people so that they act together in pursuit of an end. Sometimes leadership serves good purposes, sometimes bad; but whether the end is benign or evil, great leaders are those men and women who leave their personal stamp on history.

Now, the very concept of leadership implies the proposition that individuals can make a difference. This proposition has never been universally accepted. From classical times to the present day, eminent thinkers have regarded individuals as no more than the agents and pawns of larger forces, whether the gods and goddesses of the ancient world or, in the modern era, race, class, nation, the dialectic, the will of the people, the spirit of the times, history itself. Against such forces, the individual dwindles into insignificance.

So contends the thesis of historical determinism. Tolstoy's great novel *War and Peace* offers a famous statement of the case. Why, Tolstoy asked, did millions of men in the Napoleonic Wars, denying their human feelings and their common sense, move back and forth across Europe slaughtering their fellows? "The war," Tolstoy answered, "was bound to happen simply because it was bound to happen." All prior history predetermined it. As for leaders, they, Tolstoy said, "are but the labels that serve to give a name to an end and, like labels, they have the least possible connection with the event." The greater the leader, "the more conspicuous the inevitability and the predestination of every act he commits." The leader, said Tolstoy, is "the slave of history."

Determinism takes many forms. Marxism is the determinism of class. Nazism the determinism of race. But the idea of men and women as the slaves of history runs athwart the deepest human instincts. Rigid determinism abolishes the idea of human freedom—

the assumption of free choice that underlies every move we make, every word we speak, every thought we think. It abolishes the idea of human responsibility, since it is manifestly unfair to reward or punish people for actions that are by definition beyond their control. No one can live consistently by any deterministic creed. The Marxist states prove this themselves by their extreme susceptibility to the cult of leadership.

More than that, history refutes the idea that individuals make no difference. In December 1931 a British politician crossing Park Avenue in New York City between 76th and 77th Streets around 10:30 P.M. looked in the wrong direction and was knocked down by an automobile—a moment, he later recalled, of a man aghast, a world aglare: "I do not understand why I was not broken like an eggshell or squashed like a gooseberry." Fourteen months later an American politician, sitting in an open car in Miami, Florida, was fired on by an assassin; the man beside him was hit. Those who believe that individuals make no difference to history might well ponder whether the next two decades would have been the same had Mario Constasino's car killed Winston Churchill in 1931 and Giuseppe Zangara's bullet killed Franklin Roosevelt in 1933. Suppose, in addition, that Adolf Hitler had been killed in the street fighting during the Munich *Putsch* of 1923 and that Lenin had died of typhus during World War I. What would the 20th century be like now?

For better or for worse, individuals do make a difference. "The notion that a people can run itself and its affairs anonymously," wrote the philosopher William James, "is now well known to be the silliest of absurdities. Mankind does nothing save through initiatives on the part of inventors, great or small, and imitation by the rest of us—these are the sole factors in human progress. Individuals of genius show the way, and set the patterns, which common people then adopt and follow."

Leadership, James suggests, means leadership in thought as well as in action. In the long run, leaders in thought may well make the greater difference to the world. But, as Woodrow Wilson once said, "Those only are leaders of men, in the general eye, who lead in action. . . . It is at their hands that new thought gets its translation into the crude language of deeds." Leaders in thought often invent in solitude and obscurity, leaving to later generations the tasks of imitation. Leaders in action—the leaders portrayed in this series—have to be effective in their own time.

And they cannot be effective by themselves. They must act in response to the rhythms of their age. Their genius must be adapted, in a phrase of William James's, "to the receptivities of the moment." Leaders are useless without followers. "There goes the mob," said the French politician hearing a clamor in the streets. "I am their leader. I must follow them." Great leaders turn the inchoate emotions of the mob to purposes of their own. They seize on the opportunities of their time, the hopes, fears, frustrations, crises, potentialities. They succeed when events have prepared the way for them, when the community is awaiting to be aroused, when they can provide the clarifying and organizing ideas. Leadership ignites the circuit between the individual and the mass and thereby alters history.

It may alter history for better or for worse. Leaders have been responsible for the most extravagant follies and most monstrous crimes that have beset suffering humanity. They have also been vital in such gains as humanity has made in individual freedom, religious and racial tolerance, social justice, and respect for human rights.

There is no sure way to tell in advance who is going to lead for good and who for evil. But a glance at the gallery of men and women in *World Leaders—Past and Present* suggests some useful tests.

One test is this: Do leaders lead by force or by persuasion? By command or by consent? Through most of history leadership was exercised by the divine right of authority. The duty of followers was to defer and to obey. "Theirs not to reason why / Theirs but to do and die." On occasion, as with the so-called enlightened despots of the 18th century in Europe, absolutist leadership was animated by humane purposes. More often, absolutism nourished the passion for domination, land, gold, and conquest and resulted in tyranny.

The great revolution of modern times has been the revolution of equality. The idea that all people should be equal in their legal condition has undermined the old structure of authority, hierarchy, and deference. The revolution of equality has had two contrary effects on the nature of leadership. For equality, as Alexis de Tocqueville pointed out in his great study *Democracy in America*, might mean equality in servitude as well as equality in freedom.

"I know of only two methods of establishing equality in the political world," Tocqueville wrote. "Rights must be given to every citizen, or none at all to anyone . . . save one, who is the master of all." There was no middle ground "between the sovereignty of all and the absolute power of one man." In his astonishing prediction of 20th-century totalitarian dictatorship, Tocqueville explained how the revolution of equality could lead to the *"Führerprinzip"* and more terrible absolutism than the world had ever known.

But when rights are given to every citizen and the sovereignty of all is established, the problem of leadership takes a new form, becomes more exacting than ever before. It is easy to issue commands and enforce them by the rope and the stake, the concentration camp and the *gulag*. It is much harder to use argument and achievement to overcome opposition and win consent. The Founding Fathers of the United States understood the difficulty. They believed that history had given them the opportunity to decide, as Alexander Hamilton wrote in the first Federalist Paper, whether men are indeed capable of basing government on "reflection and choice, or whether they are forever destined to depend . . . on accident and force."

Government by reflection and choice called for a new style of leadership and a new quality of followership. It required leaders to be responsive to popular concerns, and it required followers to be active and informed participants in the process. Democracy does not eliminate emotion from politics; sometimes it fosters demagoguery; but it is confident that, as the greatest of democratic leaders put it, you cannot fool all of the people all of the time. It measures leadership by results and retires those who overreach or falter or fail.

It is true that in the long run despots are measured by results too. But they can postpone the day of judgment, sometimes indefinitely, and in the meantime they can do infinite harm. It is also true that democracy is no guarantee of virtue and intelligence in government, for the voice of the people is not necessarily the voice of God. But democracy, by assuring the right of opposition, offers built-in resistance to the evils inherent in absolutism. As the theologian Reinhold Niebuhr summed it up, "Man's capacity for justice makes democracy possible, but man's inclination to injustice makes democracy necessary."

A second test for leadership is the end for which power is sought. When leaders have as their goal the supremacy of a master race or the promotion of totalitarian revolution or the acquisition and exploitation of colonies or the protection of greed and privilege or the preservation of personal power, it is likely that their leadership will do little to advance the cause of humanity. When their goal is the abolition of slavery, the liberation of women, the enlargement of opportunity for the poor and powerless, the extension of equal rights to racial minorities, the defense of the freedoms of expression and opposition, it is likely that their leadership will increase the sum of human liberty and welfare.

Leaders have done great harm to the world. They have also conferred great benefits. You will find both sorts in this series. Even "good" leaders must be regarded with a certain wariness. Leaders are not demigods; they put on their trousers one leg after another just like ordinary mortals. No leader is infallible, and every leader needs to be reminded of this at regular intervals. Irreverence irritates leaders but is their salvation. Unquestioning submission corrupts leaders and demeans followers. Making a cult of a leader is always a mistake. Fortunately hero worship generates its own antidote. "Every hero," said Emerson, "becomes a bore at last."

The signal benefit the great leaders confer is to embolden the rest of us to live according to our own best selves, to be active, insistent, and resolute in affirming our own sense of things. For great leaders attest to the reality of human freedom against the supposed inevitabilities of history. And they attest to the wisdom and power that may lie within the most unlikely of us, which is why Abraham Lincoln remains the supreme example of great leadership. A great leader, said Emerson, exhibits new possibilities to all humanity. "We feed on genius. . . . Great men exist that there may be greater men."

Great leaders, in short, justify themselves by emancipating and empowering their followers. So humanity struggles to master its destiny, remembering with Alexis de Tocqueville: "It is true that around every man a fatal circle is traced beyond which he cannot pass; but within the wide verge of that circle he is powerful and free; as it is with man, so with communities."

1

The Communist in the Cowboy Hat

On January 28, 1979, Deng Xiaoping, the first Communist Chinese leader ever to visit the United States, arrived in Washington, D.C. The Americans had done their very best to welcome him. Lampposts all along Deng's route were bedecked with red flags, hand sewn with the five gold stars that represent the Communist party of the People's Republic of China. For weeks dignitaries and politicians had been scrambling for invitations to one of the receptions to be held for Deng. Their enthusiasm was fired by curiosity. The United States broke diplomatic relations with China in 1949, after the victory of the Communists in the civil war there, and there had been little contact between the two nations since. Now the Americans would watch Deng's every move and attempt to decipher what his visit meant for future U.S.-China relations. Perhaps the most excited participant was President Jimmy Carter. One of his aides said Carter had "been almost like a little boy preparing for this visit." Only a month earlier Carter had announced that the United States and China would normalize relations and exchange ambassadors.

Via television satellite, Chinese at home followed every detail of Deng's 9-day journey, traveling 5,500 miles with him across the United States, visiting farms, factories, and historic sights. For many in

Deng put his country style to effect, making use of the capacious spittoons in the official reception rooms to reinforce a point he was making to a visitor. . . . Such a mannerism would have been unthinkable from Zhou or from Mao.
—ROGER GARSIDE
British diplomat and historian, on Deng's political style

U.S. president Jimmy Carter greets China's leader Deng Xiaoping on the steps of the White House in January 1979. It was the first stop of Deng's nine-day tour of the United States, which underscored the restored diplomatic ties between the two nations.

Deng and his wife Zhuo Lin wave to supporters as they board a plane for the first leg of their journey to the United States. Deng's visit to the United States was the first by a top-ranking Chinese Communist leader.

Part of the entertainment arranged for Deng during his U.S. tour was a performance by the Harlem Globetrotters basketball team in Washington, D.C.

China, the television broadcasts of Deng's trip, viewed in community centers or their own homes, provided their first glimpse of the United States.

Day after day the Chinese proudly watched Deng as he made his way across the country. He proved to be adept at American-style politics. He kissed babies on their forehead, clowned with the Harlem Globetrotters basketball team, and donned a Stetson at a Texas rodeo, taking that opportunity to point out something Chinese and Americans had in common: "In Inner Mongolia," he noted, "our people are very skilled in roping wild horses." American politicians were impressed with Deng's style. Vice-president Walter Mondale told him that if he were an American citizen, his down-to-earth manner would get him elected to any office he sought.

Those who met Deng Xiaoping were astounded at his small size — only 5 feet tall — and his larger-than-life stamina. The 74 year old never seemed to tire during his trek across the United States. His enthusiasm and optimism were infectious, whether he was touring a Ford Motor plant or marveling at a rock brought back from the moon by U.S. astronauts. Few who met him would have guessed at the severe ups and downs that had marked his long political career.

Deng had weathered fierce political storms, surviving the massive upheaval of China's Cultural Revolution and the disfavor of the nation's mercurial leader, Mao Zedong, to emerge from the power struggles that followed Mao's death in 1976 as China's leader. The rapidity of his changes in fortune and the precariousness of his position during those years made Deng the subject of an often repeated joke in Beijing concerning three men in a jail cell. The first asks the second what he is in for and is told, "I opposed Deng Xiaoping." The second asks the same of the first, who says, "I supported Deng Xiaoping." Both men question the third, who tells them, "I am Deng Xiaoping." Through more than 50 years of work to bring a communist revolution to China, war with the Communists' Nationalist foes and with the nation of Japan, and years of political infighting culminating in public ridicule and exile from Communist party politics, Deng had proven himself a survivor.

Deng Xixian (he changed his name to Xiaoping after becoming a Communist and was also known at times as Deng Bin) was born in 1904 in Pai Fang, a small village in Sichuan Province, in south-central China. Because Deng has discouraged the development of the type of cult of personality that surrounded Mao Zedong, little is known about his childhood. His father, Deng Wenming, was a moderately wealthy peasant landlord who reaped a large grain harvest each year. Deng's mother, Tan (her full name is unknown), was the second of Wenming's four wives. Deng was the oldest son; he had an older sister and would ultimately have two

At Simonton, Texas, Deng was treated to a rodeo and presented with a Stetson hat. Deng's U.S. hosts marveled at his stamina and enthusiasm.

The Red Guards, the youthful vanguard of China's Cultural Revolution, wave portraits of Mao and copies of his "little red book" at a 1966 demonstration in Beijing. The Cultural Revolution was part of Communist party chairman Mao Zedong's effort to revitalize society by reviving the revolutionary fervor that had brought the Communists to power in 1949.

younger brothers, two half-sisters, and an adopted stepsister. Wenming was well known in the region, and his connections enabled him to prosper. The Deng family enjoyed a higher standard of living than most of China's peasants, who farmed extremely small plots of land rented from absentee landlords, often at the cost of a large share of the year's rice or grain crop.

Traditional Chinese society was family oriented, male dominated, and overwhelmingly agricultural. Social stability was ensured by the perpetuation of the precepts of Confucianism, the ethical philosophy derived from the teachings of the 6th- and 5th-century B.C. philosopher Confucius. Confucian thought emphasizes a stable and harmonious society based on the mutual responsibilities and obligations of individuals in fixed social relationships. Society was broken into five relationships: ruler and subject, father and son, elder brother and younger brother, husband and wife, friend and friend.

Central to Confucian philosophy was the cultivation of virtue — specifically benevolent love, righteousness, propriety, wisdom, and faithfulness. In the relationship between ruler and subject, for example, it was necessary that the ruler be virtuous and follow the path of right conduct. He was deemed to be the son of heaven, the intermediary between heaven and his subjects. As long as he ruled virtuously, he was entitled to his subjects' loyalty and obedience, and his kingdom would prosper. But should he act without virtue, he forfeited heaven's mandate. Confucius said that "when a prince's conduct is correct, his government is effective without the issuing of orders. If his personal conduct is not correct, he may issue orders but they will not be followed." An unvirtuous ruler brought disharmony between man and nature; heaven's displeasure was demonstrated by a natural calamity. The many earthquakes and floods that plagued China were often interpreted as signs that the ruling dynasty had fallen into disfavor.

Deng grew up during a crucial period in Chinese history. China had been ruled by a succession of imperial dynasties, the oldest dating back approx-

imately 4,000 years, but by the early 1900s the Qing, or Manchu, dynasty was in its death throes, unable to combat both Western infiltration and internal unrest. From the 16th century onward traders from the Western nations — primarily Portugal, Spain, Great Britain, France, the Netherlands, and Russia — came to China, drawn by silk, spices, and other products. The proud Chinese viewed the outsiders as inferior and barbaric and sought to limit contact, but from the outset it was evident that the Western nations possessed superior technology and military strength. In the late 17th and early 18th centuries Europe underwent its industrial revolution, which greatly enhanced the European nations' productive capacities, increased their wealth, made possible still further technological innovations, and fired their desire for trading partners and markets. Contact with China increased, as did the attempts

A peasant carries water buckets on a farm overlooking Mao's childhood home in Hunan Province, which was maintained by the government as a museum. As China's leader, Deng avoided the type of cult of personality that developed around Mao.

by the Qing dynasty emperors to dictate the terms of that contact. The most important measure sought to limit Western trade to the port at Guangzhou (Canton).

In the early 1800s opium smoking became increasingly prevalent in China. By the 1830s it is estimated that as many as 10 million Chinese were addicted to the drug, and this captive market ensured hefty profits for opium traders. Britain, determined to expand its trade with China, was able to obtain virtually unlimited supplies of opium from India, then a British colony and the drug's chief producer. The Qing emperor's attempts to stop the British opium trade resulted in war in November 1839, but the poorly trained and uninspired Chinese forces were no match for Britain's gunships. Britain was victorious in 1842 and forced China to sign a treaty opening five Chinese cities to British trade and residence. Other European nations and the United States quickly followed suit, negotiating what became known as the "unequal treaties" with the Chinese.

The most important provisions of the unequal treaties allowed the Western nations trade access to Chinese ports as well as the right to establish settlements there. As the treaties granted the Western nations *extraterritoriality*, that is, legal jurisdiction over their citizens in China, the settlements, or concessions, were essentially governed and administered by Western consuls or trade representatives. The "most-favored nation" clauses of the treaties guaranteed that any privileges granted to one nation would be granted to all. Gradually the Western nations extended their influence from the treaty ports inland, so that by the end of the 19th century much of China had been carved into spheres of influence under European domination.

For centuries the Chinese had viewed China as an oasis of civilization surrounded by barbarians. They called their country *Zhong Guo*, or "Middle Kingdom." But the ascendancy of the West in China highlighted the weakness of the Qing dynasty emperors. The inability of the Qings to expel the foreigners suggested to the Chinese that their rulers

A Chinese opium parlor in 1906. Seeking new markets, the British introduced the opium trade to China in the early 1800s. Attempts by China's emperors to regulate the trade led to war. The British scored a decisive victory, and opium addiction became widespread.

had lost heaven's blessing, while the oppressive taxation of the late Qing period and the widespread corruption and graft of its officials provided explanations for why this might be so. Meanwhile, other forces were bringing pressure to bear on China's social order. The relative stability and prosperity China had enjoyed in the 17th and 18th centuries under the Qings contributed to a quadrupling of the nation's population between 1750 and 1850. China was heavily agricultural, with most of its population peasants; virtually all of its arable land was already under cultivation. The population boom increased the pressure on the land and the vulnerability of the peasantry to the frequent floods, earthquakes, and famines. As land was traditionally divided among all of a man's sons at his death, plots grew smaller and smaller. While the Industrial Revolution in Europe created new wealth and job opportunities, China did not undergo any comparable industrialization and remained dependent on agriculture and foreign trade. Many peasants did not own their own land but rented from wealthy landowning families. From these wealthy families came the *mandarins*, or scholar-gentry, who obtained their positions as the bureaucrats and officeholders of the imperial administration by passing examinations on the Confucian classics. As the standard of living of the peasants declined, their resentment toward the landlords and the mandarins increased.

The restlessness of the peasantry manifested itself in the Taiping Rebellion, led by Hung Xiuchan (a three-time failure at the government examinations) who claimed divine inspiration and preached

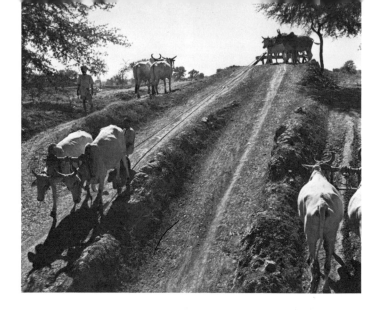

In Deng's youth the peasantry composed the overwhelming majority of China's population. Then, as now, most farming was done according to time-honored methods, using livestock and traditional implements rather than machinery.

his own version of Christianity leavened with collective ownership and decision making. The Taiping Rebellion broke out in July 1850 and by October 1854 had gained millions of adherents, mostly among the peasants and other disaffected elements of Chinese society; established itself in 16 of the country's 18 provinces; and come within 30 miles of the capital, Beijing (Peking). Over the next 10 years imperial and European forces subdued the rebellion, at an estimated cost of 20 million lives.

Chinese discontent focused on the Western presence as well as the Qing dynasty. In 1900 a secret society known as the Righteous and Harmonious Fists, or Boxers, attacked foreign legations and Christian missionaries in Beijing before being put down by forces from several Western nations.

In the early years of Deng's life the most important force for change in China was the *Zhongguo Tong Meng Hui* (Chinese United League) headed by Sun Yat-sen, who had dedicated himself to overthrowing the Qings and establishing a socialist, republican government. Reform efforts by the Qing rulers were too late, and in February 1912 the last Qing emperor, the six-year-old Xuantung (later known in the West as Henry Pu-yi) abdicated. Sun, who had been chosen provisional president in November 1911, resigned and offered the position to Yuan Shikai, a military leader supported by most of the armed forces and Great Britain.

By the time Deng reached school age, the ancient

examination system had been abolished. New schools were being established, many based on Japanese models, which in turn had been based on the European system. Deng enrolled in one of the new "progressive" schools and apparently progressed satisfactorily with his studies, because his father later sent him to Chongqing Preparatory School, one of the best secondary schools in Sichuan. Through his classmates in the city of Chongqing he learned about the events that were changing his country. Like them, he became concerned about the future of China.

World War I was fought from 1914 to 1918 and pitted the Western Allies — including Britain, France, Italy, Russia, and the United States — against the Central Powers — Germany, Austria-Hungary, and the Ottoman Empire (Turkey). Although little fighting took place in East Asia, Japan supported the Allies and moved into the German-leased city of Tsingtao, on China's Shandong Peninsula. Japan then pressed upon Yuan Shikai a list of 21 demands calling for an extension of Japanese privileges in China. The Twenty-One Demands also required that China buy all military material from Japan, come to Japan for all loans, appoint Japanese economic and military advisers, and turn over China's iron industry to the Japanese. Since the Western nations had ended Japan's self-imposed isolation in 1854, Japan had modernized and greatly strengthened itself, and it was now determined to become the equal of any Western power. In comparison China was still underdeveloped and

These Chinese troops served under British commander Charles Gordon, who helped China's ineffectual Qing dynasty emperors quell the massive Taiping Rebellion. The uprising lasted from 1850 to 1864 and was the first manifestation of the peasantry's discontent.

backward. Yuan Shikai's government was having difficulty establishing its authority, and China was powerless to resist the Japanese. Although the demands were somewhat modified in their final form, they compromised China's sovereignty and were an affront to patriotic Chinese.

President Woodrow Wilson of the United States said that World War I was being fought to make the world safe for democracy, and with the overthrow of Russia's royal dynasty in March 1917, it was possible to see the war as a conflict between the West's enlightened democracies and the outdated and repressive monarchies of the Central Powers. Wilson's war aims were spelled out in the Fourteen Points, which seemed to promise a degree of self-determination to colonial nations such as China. Yuan Shikai had arrogated power to himself (he aspired to become emperor) and driven Sun Yat-sen into opposition and exile in Japan. After Yuan's death in June 1916, China was controlled by regional military commanders, known as warlords, but there was still much republican sentiment, and many Chinese hoped that the victorious Allies would redress the Twenty-One Demands, force Japan to leave the Shandong Peninsula, and moderate their own exploitation of China.

The Paris peace talks were a great disappointment to the Chinese. The Allies announced in April 1919 that Japan would be allowed to remain in the Shandong Peninsula. On May 4 thousands of Chinese marched in protest of the decision. Deng and other students at the Chongqing Preparatory School took part in the demonstration, which proved to be the greatest exhibition of Chinese nationalism to that point. Anti-Japanese boycotts were announced, a general strike was called, and the Chinese government was forced to announce that it would not sign the peace treaty. The Allied decision to apportion the losers' former colonies in Africa and the Middle East among themselves further demonstrated to the Chinese that the democracies were only paying lip service to the idea of self-determination while actually continuing their policy of colonialism. The Allied refusal to include a clause in the final peace treaty proclaiming the racial equality of nations confirmed that the West believed itself superior.

Despite the betrayal at the Paris peace conference, many Chinese students were still drawn to the West. Educated Chinese recognized that their country was weak and undeveloped and looked to the European nations for ideas on how to modernize. France was a favorite destination of Chinese students, who hoped that they would benefit from the technological advancements of the industrialized countries. After graduating from the Chongqing school in September 1920, the 16-year-old Deng traveled with 90 other students to France. It was Deng's first trip outside of Sichuan Province. Many years later he would tell the *New York Times*, "We felt that China was weak and we wanted to make her strong. We thought that the way to do it was through modernization. So we went to the West to learn."

Like most of the European nations, France suffered a severe economic recession after the war, which made it difficult for the Chinese students to find jobs. Deng worked with 150 other students in an arms factory and later took a job in a shoe factory south of Paris.

It was in France that Deng became a Communist. As formulated in the work of the 19th-century German economist and historian Karl Marx, communism held that class struggle was the crucial element of history. In industrialized capitalist democracies like those of the West, Marx perceived a class struggle between the *bourgeoisie*, who owned the means of production, and the *proletariat*, or industrial working class. Capitalism (the economic system based on private ownership), Marx argued, was inherently unjust. Because the small bourgeoisie class controlled the means of production, namely the factories, it reaped all of the profits for itself while paying the workers only enough to subsist. Capitalism, then, contained the seeds of its own destruction in that ultimately the workers would develop class consciousness, become aware of the inequitable distribution of wealth, and rise up to smash the bourgeoisie and the state. The workers

When the six-year-old emperor Xuantung (later known as Henry Pu-yi) abdicated in February 1912, it marked the end of more than 2,000 years of imperial rule in China. The new government was headed by Sun Yat-sen, who hoped to establish a socialist, parliamentary democracy.

Sun resigned the presidency in favor of Yuan Shikai, a military leader supported by Great Britain. Yuan had little understanding of democracy and no tolerance for dissent, and his dictatorial arrogation of power soon drove Sun into opposition.

would then establish a classless society, with collective ownership of industry and property and equal distribution of wealth. Although Marx believed it was necessary that countries pass through capitalism as a phase of their historical development, he also held that its destruction was historically inevitable.

Deng had widespread exposure to Marxist thought while in France, where there was an active and well-organized socialist party led by Léon Blum. (The socialists differed from the communists primarily in their belief that socialism or communism could be achieved not only by violent revolution but through participation in the democratic political process.) Much political talk in France concerned Russia, where the Bolsheviks, Russia's communist party, had taken power in November 1917 and established the world's first communist state. The Russian Revolution provided an answer to the question of how a communist revolution might succeed in China, which was neither a democracy nor industrialized and possessed only a very small proletariat. Most Chinese were peasants, and Marx, unlike Mao later, did not consider the peasantry a potential revolutionary force. Russia had been in many ways similar. It had a long history of autocracy under the tsars, and although more developed economically than China, Russia's population was also mostly peasants. The leader of the Bolsheviks, Vladimir Lenin, expanded on Marx's work and proposed that a secret, well-disciplined party could make a communist revolution even though historical conditions were not yet right. The success of the Bolsheviks seemed to confirm Lenin's theories.

To Deng and other young Chinese disillusioned with the West and discouraged by China's failed attempts at reform, communism promised an answer to the poverty of the peasantry and the economic injustices that were China's greatest problems. Chinese still at home were exposed to the same exciting ideas from Russia. As China continued to be the object of economic exploitation by the West, educated Chinese were intrigued by Lenin's analysis of imperialism, which he called the "highest form of capitalism," and were impressed when the Bolshevik government promised to annul Russia's unequal treaties with China. In July 1921 Mao Zedong and 11 other Chinese met secretly in the French concession of Shanghai and formed the Chinese Communist party (CCP). One year later Deng joined the French Communist party.

It was through his involvement with the party that Deng met Zhou Enlai, a fellow student who had arrived in France two months after him. Zhou, whom Henry Kissinger would later call "the greatest statesman of our era," immediately displayed his talents as a political organizer by establishing a branch of the CCP in France. Deng did clerical work for its first official publication, *Red Glow*, which Zhou edited.

Zhou did not confine his work to France. He made contact with other expatriate Chinese. In Berlin, Germany, he recruited Zhu De, another native of Sichuan. Zhu was about 40 years old and had received Western military training at the Yunnan Military Academy. He had fought with the republican forces that overthrew the Qings, only to revolt against Yuan Shikai and his imperial ambitions. During the heyday of the warlords after the death of Yuan, Zhu was a provincial official. Dissatisfied with the state of China, Zhu resigned his post and traveled first to Shanghai, where he associated with student groups, then to Germany, where he met Zhou and other Chinese Communists.

Deng went back to China in 1926. Many of the Chinese students who were returning to their country at this time were prepared to support the CCP. Deng, Zhou, and Zhu, along with Mao Zedong, a peasant from Hunan who had never left China, would provide the CCP with a core of leadership for the next six decades.

2

"The Little Cannon"

In the summer of 1912 Sun Yat-sen had renamed the Chinese United League the *Guomindang*, which means Nationalist party. After Yuan's death, Sun had returned from Japan and allied himself with warlords in the south of China, in and around Guangzhou. Each warlord administered the area under his control, collecting taxes and providing a crude kind of law and order. Clashes among them were frequent, as they sought to expand their influence or maintain their control. Foreign governments generally recognized as China's government whichever warlord controlled Beijing. In the south Sun attempted to establish his own government and campaign against the northern warlords, but he had no army of his own and was dependent on southern warlords for military support.

Marxist doctrine held that the communist revolution was to be a worldwide movement, transcending national boundaries and racial and ethnic differences. The proletariat in all countries had the same vital interest — to smash capitalism — and this goal transcended nationalism, which was an outgrowth of the capitalist economic structure. The Union of Soviet Socialist Republics (as Russia had renamed itself in 1917) was thus bound on supporting communist and revolutionary movements in other nations, a determination reinforced by the

The real trouble is that China is not an independent country. She is the victim of foreign countries.
—SUN YAT-SEN
Chinese statesman and revolutionary leader

The father of the Chinese republic, Sun Yat-sen founded the Guomindang, or Nationalist Party, in 1912 as a vehicle for his ambitions. His political philosophy was based on his "Three Principles of the People": nationalism, democracy, and social well-being.

Sun with his troops in Shanghai, 1912. Sun made alliances with southern warlords (regional military governors) in order to continue his struggle with Yuan and his successors.

invasion of the Soviet Union after World War I by 50,000 Allied troops bent on overthrowing the Bolsheviks.

The Chinese Communists quite naturally looked to the Soviet Union for leadership. While Deng was in France, the CCP was instructed by the Soviets to cooperate with the Guomindang. The Soviets supported the Guomindang because although it was not Marxist in orientation, it was the most legitimate revolutionary force in China. The CCP was still small, and the Guomindang enjoyed more broad-based support.

Soviet assistance enabled the Guomindang to establish a military academy on Huangpu Island, near Guangzhou. Zhou Enlai was made responsible for the political education of its students, while Chiang Kai-shek took charge of military training. Chiang had traveled to Moscow in 1923; his trip convinced him that the Soviet Union had territorial ambitions in China and was interested only in dominating the CCP. When Sun died of cancer in March 1925, Chiang emerged as his successor.

After Sun's death the Soviets established a university in his name in Moscow. Both CCP and Guomindang members were trained there, and many of the Chinese students in Europe spent time at the Sun Yat-sen University on their way home. Deng arrived there in January 1926. He took courses in Russian, Marxist theory, and military strategy. As he had in France, the able young man with the small but sturdy frame and the abrupt and forthright manner impressed his classmates. They called him "the little cannon."

Feng Yuxian was a warlord who controlled most of China's northwest provinces. He was known as the Christian General, and it was said he baptized his troops with a fire hose. Having lost territory to rival warlords, he came to Moscow seeking military aid and within days joined the Guomindang and pledged to devote himself to a united China. In return he received aid from the Soviets and the services of CCP, Guomindang, and Soviet military advisers to help rebuild his army. Deng Xiaoping was among the CCP members with whom Feng chose to return to China.

After swearing an oath of allegiance to the Guomindang, Feng and his advisers began the reorganization of his sizable army. A military academy in Shanxi Province was established to provide Feng with trained soldiers, and Deng was named the dean. The army had to be ideologically indoctrinated as well as taught military skills. The soldiers were taught Sun Yat-sen's three principles of socialism, nationalism, and democracy as well as a heavy dose of Marxist theory.

Chiang's distrust of the Communists grew. In 1926 more than one-third of the delegates to the Guomindang congress at Guangzhou were Communists. Chiang also found himself opposed by many in the Guomindang leadership who were not Communists, including Sun's widow (and Chiang's future sister-in-law), Soong Ching-ling, and Sun's longtime associate Wang Jingwei.

In the spring of 1927 a general strike led by Zhou and other Communists shut down Shanghai, and the Communists took control of the city. When Chiang ordered the armed pickets to lay down their arms, they complied, expecting that the Guomindang army would take command, but the Nationalists turned on the Communists and their sympathizers. The Communist leaders were ar-

Chiang Kai-shek, shown at the gate of the Ming dynasty tombs in 1927, emerged as the head of the Guomindang after Sun's death in March 1925. Subsequent military victories over the warlords enabled Chiang to claim the leadership of a unified China.

Deng's first important work for the Chinese Communist party (CCP) was providing political education to the troops of Feng Yuxian (pictured), a northern warlord who allied himself with the Guomindang in 1924.

rested or executed. Chiang offered the equivalent of $200,000 for the capture of Zhou, who managed to escape. Thousands of Communists were killed. Similar events took place in other cities. The surviving Communists were purged from the Guomindang. Recognizing that he was outmatched, Feng went over to Chiang, as did Wang Jingwei. Deng and 50 other Communists were expelled from Feng's army, but they were fortunate to escape the executions that were the fate of many of their comrades. With no military support, the CCP was on the verge of being wiped out.

The CCP leadership met on August 7 in Hankou, one of the three small cities that form the metropolis of Wuhan. There, Deng met Mao Zedong for the first time. While Mao insisted that it was the peasants who were the true revolutionary force in China, the CCP had pursued a more orthodox Marxist line and concentrated on organizing the urban workers. Mao had spent much of the previous two years directing the Guomindang's Peasant Movement Training Institute and organizing the peasants in his native Hunan Province. In March 1927 he published his *Report of an Investigation on the Peasant Movement in Hunan*, which asserted that China's peasants were ready to create their own revolution. "In a very short time, in China's central, southern and northern provinces," Mao wrote, "several hundred million peasants will rise like a mighty storm, like a hurricane, a force so swift and violent that no power, however great, will be able to hold it back." The challenge for the Communists, Mao said, was to decide whether they were prepared to lead the peasantry.

The CCP leadership was not ready to accept Mao's message. Their attention remained focused on the cities. Zhou came to the meeting fresh from leading a failed uprising at the city of Nanchang. Mao was directed to foment a rebellion at Changsha, the largest city in Hunan. Other operations were directed at other cities, but the Autumn Harvest Uprisings (they were timed to coincide with the gathering of the autumn harvest) were a dismal failure. The poorly trained and ill-equipped Communist forces were no match for the Guomindang armies. Mao retreated with 400 ragged survivors of the Hunan operation to Jinggangshan, a mountainous region along the border of Hunan and Jiangxi provinces, where he could put his ideas into practice with a minimum of interference from the CCP leadership.

Deng went to Shanghai, where he worked underground, rebuilding the shattered CCP cells. There he fell in love and married Zhang Qianyuan, a dedicated party member from Jiangxi. Attracted by the party's message of sexual equality, many women became CCP cadres. Women in Chinese society had limited freedom. A son was considered a greater blessing to a family than a daughter, and a woman was expected to be subservient to her brothers, her male children, and her husband. Marriages were arranged by parents, and a woman's greatest value was as a laborer and childbearer. The ancient custom of foot binding, whereby an infant girl's feet were bound to prevent growth (small feet were considered more beautiful and desirable), caused terrible mutilation and served the ancillary purpose of limiting a woman's independence. Mao wrote many

Mao (standing, third from left) posed in 1937 with other veterans of the Autumn Harvest Uprising of 1927. Mao opposed the CCP leadership's emphasis on urban-based rebellion. After the failure of the uprising, he retreated to the mountains of Jinggangshan with about 400 men to organize the peasantry.

articles encouraging increased rights for women and denouncing the practice of arranged marriage. It was the role of women, Mao said, to "hold up half the sky."

With the Guomindang now in control of most of southern and central China, Chiang embarked on an expedition against the northern warlords and occupied Beijing in June 1928. When the warlord of Manchuria (China's three northeastern provinces), the "Young Marshal," Zhang Xueliang, declared his allegiance to the Guomindang, Chiang's government could claim control of all China. He established his capital at Nanjing, and foreign powers recognized the Nationalist regime as China's government.

Mao had great success in his mountain redoubt in Jinggangshan, where he was soon joined by Zhu De, now a commander of some renown; Peng Dehuai, a former Guomindang general; and the brilliant young officer Lin Biao. He initiated land reform programs, taking land from the wealthier landlords and redistributing it among the peasants. The peasants were also given political education lessons. Mao told his own soldiers that in order to win the revolution it would be necessary to win the loyalty of the peasantry, and he taught them his famous rules of guerrilla warfare. The Communists in Jinggang-

Peasants trundle a cartload of coffins in Guangzhou (Canton) in December 1927. Hundreds of civilians were killed there during fighting between CCP forces and Nationalist troops after a Communist rebellion.

shan soon established their own government, or soviet, in Jiangxi. At the party's sixth congress, held in Moscow in the summer of 1928, the CCP grudgingly acknowledged Mao's success and the legitimacy of his methods. The "Mao-Zhu Army," as it was called by the peasants, was recognized as the Fourth Red Army. Moscow still wished to emphasize organizational work in the cities, and Li Lisan and Qu Quibai, adherents of the Moscow line, emerged as the party's leaders.

At the congress, Deng was named deputy secretary-general of the CCP. The following year he was sent to Guangxi Province, in the southwest near Vietnam, to try to gain recruits for the Red Army. He infiltrated the military of the southern warlord Li Zongren and set up clandestine Communist cells within Li's forces. Deng and his comrades were quickly able to position 300 Communist party members within his army, laying the foundations for a Red Army in Guangxi. Soon some of these men were in positions of leadership.

Li Zongren had his differences with the Nationalist government. Like other warlords, he wanted to maintain a degree of independence in his territory.

Nationalist soldiers under attack in October 1928. Chiang's assertions that he headed a unified central government were belied by civil war with the Communists and the refusal of his former warlord allies to disarm.

French photojournalist Henri Cartier-Bresson captured this image of Hung Kwei, one of the last of the great warlords. American journalists Theodore White and Annalee Jacoby wrote: "The great warlords governed entire provinces. . . . Their will was law; paper they printed was money . . . foul play became the code of Chinese politics."

Initially Chiang had gone along with the demands of Li Zongren and the other so-called new warlords who had consolidated their power in different parts of China after the Nationalist revolution. However, as the central government established itself, Chiang tried to persuade the warlords to disarm. This would centralize power in the national government, which commanded over 2 million troops. The warlords in Guangxi, Li among them, were unwilling to surrender their power base. In April 1929 Chiang attacked the Guangxi forces. Through a subterfuge, Deng and the small Red Army he had created in Guangxi were able to avoid combat. They retreated by boat up the Yu River to the small town of Diendung, where they established a government. On a drizzly morning in December 1930 Deng and his military commander Zhang Yunyi each made a short speech before the assembled army and local civilians, proclaiming the establishment of the Seventh Red Army. Deng was appointed its political commissar.

In February 1930 the Yu River Soviet was established. As its political commissar, Deng Xiaoping began to experiment with land reform. He was impressed by what Mao Zedong had achieved in Jiangxi. He also established a collective farm where the land and livestock were jointly owned by the commune members.

There would be little time for peaceful experimentation, however. Taking his cue from Moscow, Li Lisan encouraged direct attacks on the Nationalist forces. Chiang Kai-shek was having troubles with Feng Yuxian and other rebellious warlords who were still unhappy with his disarmament plans. Wang Jingwei had returned to China from exile in Europe to reorganize the Guomindang's left wing and claimed that Chiang was an incipient dictator concerned only with making China his personal fiefdom. Feng and Chiang were soon at war. Despite the opposition of Mao and others, who believed that the Communists were not strong enough to carry out anything but guerrilla actions, Li Lisan ordered an offensive. Troops in the south were ordered to march on Wuhan and other cities. Deng worried

Like Deng, Lin Biao was one of Mao's earliest supporters. As Mao took control of the CCP, Lin's star rose. A brilliant military commander who was said never to have lost a battle, Lin was officially proclaimed "Mao's closest comrade-in-arms" in 1966, but he later ran afoul of the chairman.

that the departure of the Seventh and Eighth armies from the newly formed soviets in the south would leave those areas unprotected, but he did not want to contradict Li Lisan's policy. The Guangxi soviet was attacked and fell to the Nationalists soon after the Seventh Army's departure. The invasion of Wuhan proved premature. Of the 20,000 troops in the Seventh and Eighth armies, only 6,000 survived. Deng was faulted by the CCP for uncritically following the "Li Lisan line." What was left of the Seventh Army made its way to Jiangxi and joined Mao's forces there.

Deng was sent to Shanghai and remained there as the assistant to Zhou Enlai. In Shanghai, Deng's wife, Zhang Qianyuan, died as a result of a miscarriage. Deng had little time to mourn either his personal loss or the undoing of his work in Guangxi. Like most of the Communists, Deng's first commitment was to the revolution, and there was still much work to be done.

3

Revolutionary Odyssey

In January 1932 Deng Xiaoping was sent to Jiangxi, where for the first time he worked closely with Mao Zedong. Much of the CCP politburo (the party's executive committee) had moved from Shanghai to Jiangxi, and the market city of Ruijin became the CCP's most important base. While the CCP debated tactics and strengthened its stronghold in Jiangxi, Chiang launched a series of "annihilation campaigns" against the Communists.

Mao was engaged in his own struggle against the politburo members from Shanghai, many of whom still disagreed with his approach. The 28 Bolsheviks, a group of theorists who had just arrived from the Sun Yat-sen University, were a special thorn in Mao's side. Led by Bo Gu, they believed that the Communists should be more aggressive and take the war to the Nationalists by attacking and seeking to expand their territory.

Mao believed such thinking misguided and ignorant of the specific conditions in China. "A revolution," he wrote, "does not march a straight line. It wanders where it can, retreats before superior forces, advances wherever it has room, attacks whenever the enemy retreats or bluffs and, above all, is possessed of enormous patience." The Communists were still outnumbered and outgunned by the Nationalists, and to engage them in pitched

The Nationalists opposed communism partly for generational reasons. Most of them were older than the Communists, who had come of age during the May Fourth Movement. . . . For the older generation, Russia remained just another country not to be trusted, and May Fourth was school boy rowdyism.
—ED HAMMOND
historian

Mao was photographed in 1936 in an airfield not far from Yanan. The Communists established their new capital there at the conclusion of the Long March, a heroic 6,000-mile strategic retreat to avoid encirclement by Chiang's forces.

combat was folly. A wiser strategy would be to remain mobile and willing to sacrifice territory in order to lure the Guomindang forces into unfamiliar areas, where the Communists could use hit-and-run tactics against them. Mao's success at Jinggangshan and in Jiangxi also left him convinced of the absolute correctness of his view that it was the peasants who were the key to the revolution's success.

Mao had enough support to be made chairman of the Central Executive Committee of the Soviet Republic of China, but the 28 Bolsheviks controlled the politburo, and their policies became the official party line. Mao was head of state, but it was a state that controlled little territory and was not acknowledged by most foreign governments. At the time Mao's name was not even recognizable to most of his countrymen.

Deng believed that if a tactic worked it was by definition a good tactic, a practical viewpoint that led him to favor Mao's guerrilla strategy. Mao's success in repelling Chiang's first three annihilation campaigns proved the soundness of his strategies to Deng. He became one of Mao's closest political and personal allies and a staunch defender of his policies.

In Ruijin, Deng was first made secretary of the district party committee but soon assumed more important duties as the secretary of the party committee for the entire province. An important aspect of Deng's new position was the reunification of the party, which had been divided by political infighting and factional disputes giving rise to charges of counterrevolution and betrayal. Claiming that the Red Army had been infiltrated by Guomindang secret agents, Mao ordered more than 4,000 of its officers and soldiers arrested. Torture was used to obtain confessions, and several thousand prisoners were executed. A mutiny at the city of Fukien was dealt with in similar fashion by Mao. Although Mao said he initially acted on evidence uncovered by Zhu, critics charged that the alleged infiltration was merely a pretext for Mao to eliminate his opponents

Weapons are an important factor in war, but not the decisive factor; it is people, not things, that are decisive. The contest of strength is not only a contest of human power and morale. Military and economic power is necessarily wielded by people.

—MAO ZEDONG
revolutionary and leader of
China from 1949 to 1976

within the party. A meeting of the CCP Central Committee in Shanghai in January 1931 was marked by an unusually bitter dispute between the 28 Bolsheviks and some of their opponents, who angrily left the meeting and were arrested shortly afterward and executed by the Guomindang. It was charged that the 28 Bolsheviks had informed on them. Finally, in early 1931 Zhou's chief of security, Gu Shunzhang, defected to the Guomindang and provided information that led to the arrest of 800 Communists. Zhou himself narrowly escaped capture, and in retaliation he ordered the murder of Gu's entire family.

Deng worked to help the party heal its wounds. As his political prospects improved, romance returned to his life. Deng and Jin Weiying, his successor at the district party committee, were married after a brief courtship. For a short time the couple, devoted to one another and to their cause, worked together at the provincial party committee, but the dilemmas that continued to divide the party soon ended their marriage.

Mao's situation in Jiangxi had begun to deteriorate. When Chiang launched his fourth annihila-

China's huge population has cultivated virtually all of the nation's arable land for agricultural purposes. The Communists showed the peasants in Shanxi Province how to utilize terraces to increase grain production and protect against erosion.

tion campaign, the politburo once again insisted that the Communists carry the battle to the Nationalists. Luo Ming, one of Mao's supporters, was threatened by Nationalist attack in a nearby province. When he pointed out that his army was not strong enough to repel the Nationalists and resorted to guerrilla tactics, the 28 Bolsheviks denounced him and his supporters, including Deng, for their "defeatist" line. Deng may have had a chance to save himself by denouncing Mao and Luo Ming, but he stuck to his beliefs. His wife supported the politburo's policy and divorced him, thus protecting her own career.

The anti–Luo Ming campaign was the first of the famous three purges that Deng would survive in his long political career. He was removed from his political posts, forced to write self-criticisms, and demoted to an academic position at the Red Army Academy. It was over a decade before the charges against him were officially cleared.

The military situation grew worse for the Communists. In the summer of 1934 Chiang, assisted by two German generals, Hans von Seecht and Alexander von Falkenhausen, initiated his fifth annihilation campaign and directed nearly 1 million troops against the CCP base areas in Jiangxi. Mao urged retreat, arguing that the Communists could establish new soviets elsewhere, but the 28 Bolsheviks, Zhou, and the CCP's own German military adviser, Otto Braun, argued that the party should not surrender its bases. The Communists were soon surrounded. In October 1934, 100,000 Red Army soldiers and party cadres broke through the Nationalist encirclement and marched west. Mao said that when the Communists embarked on the famed Long March they had no destination in mind but were seeking only to escape the Nationalists. Ahead was a 6,000-mile trek — in essence a running battle — that is one of the greatest feats of modern history. Although the Long March has come to be seen as a symbol of the dedication and fortitude of the Chinese Communists, at the time it must have seemed an ignominious retreat. Many of the Communists were forced to leave behind family members

Deng Xiaoping started the Long March under a dark cloud. He had been removed from his army and political posts, had been harshly "struggled against," had been held under armed guard and publicly denounced, and his wife had divorced him.

—HARRISON E. SALISBURY
American historian

who were too young or old for the journey. Those remaining behind faced probable murder, torture, or imprisonment at the hands of the Guomindang.

Deng was 30 when he set off on the Long March. Because of his support for Luo Ming, Deng began the march as a soldier, not an officer. He brought with him only what he could carry on his back, but he was fortunate to be allowed to go at all. Most of those compelled to remain behind were Mao's supporters. Mao's brother Zetan, who was the same age as Deng, remained in Jiangxi and was captured and executed just a few months after the departure of the Red Army. Mao's two infant sons were too young to travel and were left with trustworthy families in Jiangxi. Mao searched for the children later, but they were never heard from again.

Once the Communists were free of the Nationalist encirclement, Braun and the 28 Bolsheviks urged that they stand and fight. Mao disagreed. He believed that the Communists should keep on the move and use guerrilla tactics to harass and demoralize the Nationalists. While retreating, the Communists could work with the peasants in the areas they passed through, and their discipline and dedication would win them supporters and recruits, as had occurred in Jiangxi.

Fewer than 10 percent of the 100,000 CCP soldiers and cadres who embarked on the Long March in October 1934 made it to Shaanxi Province, where the Communists finally halted one year later. These ragged survivors were members of the Second Front Army, whose journey was said to have been even more grueling than that of the main body of the Red Army.

Marching westward, the Communists reached the Xiang River in December. Half of their number were able to cross before the entire column came under Nationalist attack. Almost half of the Red Army troops were killed or so severely wounded that they could not continue the march. Mao argued that the army's progress had been slowed due to Bo's insistence on transporting printing presses and other heavy equipment from Jiangxi.

At a January 1935 meeting at Zunyi, in Guizhou Province, Mao attacked the 28 Bolsheviks and Zhou for their policies, which he said were responsible for the Communists' losses. Displaying the adaptability and skill at conciliation that was to become his trademark, Zhou agreed, saying that Mao had been "right all the time and we should listen to him." The Bolsheviks and Braun were discredited, and Mao was made a member of the politburo and chairman of the military council. From that point on he would often be referred to as Chairman Mao. For all intents and purposes he was now the military and political leader of the Communists, and his concept of defensive guerrilla war was adopted as the party's policy.

At Zunyi, Mao also determined that the official party line would be that the Communists were not retreating but marching north to combat the Japanese, who had invaded and occupied Manchuria in 1931. The CCP policy of unyielding opposition to the Japanese won it many supporters. Patriotic Chinese had grown increasingly resentful of foreign exploitation and bristled at the Japanese invasion. While the Communists had immediately declared war on the Japanese in 1931 and proposed a united front with the Nationalists to resist the invaders, many Chinese believed that Chiang was willing to accommodate the Japanese and was more concerned with fighting the Communists. Mao and the Communists were thus able to use the patriotic sentiment that had been growing in China since the early 1900s to benefit their own cause.

Deng's diminished status at the time of the Zunyi meeting is indicated by the fact that years afterward some of its participants could not recall whether he had attended. Zhou was always positive that Deng had been there, and documents discovered by Chinese historians in 1984 proved that Deng had indeed taken part in the famous meeting, most likely as recording secretary. Deng's support for the victorious Mao greatly improved his circumstances, and when the Communists left Zunyi, Deng no longer marched but rode a horse, a privilege reserved for the more important party leaders and military officers.

From Zunyi the Communists moved west and then north, reversed directions, then went north again. Guizhou and Sichuan provinces were warlord territory, and Guomindang forces were also in the area. Mao split his forces, marched in one direction and then the next, and feinted toward towns and cities to keep Chiang uncertain about where the Communists were headed next. Once Chiang committed his forces, Mao moved, usually in strategic retreat. The Communist forces were often bombed by Guomindang aircraft. Under Guomindang bombardment at the River of the Golden Sands, the Communists climbed poorly marked, winding paths through steep hills and were able to cross the river with minimal casualties, temporarily putting the river between themselves and their pursuers. Farther north 22 members of a Red Army advance squad swung hand over hand across an iron chain bridge at Luding to knock out a Nationalist machine-gun emplacement on the far side. Their heroism enabled Mao to take his 13,000 remaining troops across the Dadu River and finally escape Chiang's pursuit. The Communists pressed northward. Hundreds died from the cold and the thin altitude while crossing the Great Snowy Mountains. Beyond the Snowies, in western China, they were ambushed by Tibetan tribesmen, inheritors of a centuries-old hatred of the Chinese. China's western grasslands were an eerie, deserted marsh. Some of the exhausted marchers were simply swallowed up by the bog, and others perished of malnourishment, fatigue, and dehydration. Most depressing of all, according to survivors, was the utter emptiness of the western areas, whose few inhabitants had deserted their villages at hearing that the Chinese approached. The Communists on the Long March were mostly from heavily populated southern China, and they found the desolate grasslands haunting and frightening. One of the physicians on the Long March speculated that many of the deaths in the grasslands were from despair.

The Long March came to an end in northern Shaanxi Province in October 1935, one year after it had begun. Fewer than 10,000 Communists survived the trek; those who had would form the nucleus of the Communist party for years to come. Deng was stricken with typhoid fever during the later stages of the march and may have been among those who arrived in Shaanxi on a stretcher.

Mao felt that the Long March was both a victory and a defeat. The hard work that went into establishing the Chinese Soviet Republic had all been undone, but the Long March had enabled the Communists to survive — albeit in greatly reduced numbers — to fight another day. The march had taken the Communists more than 6,000 miles through 11 provinces; in many of the provinces the Communists had carried out land reform and political education programs. The Long March enabled the Communists to disseminate their message across a

Peasants press against army barricades in 1938 to demand food from the Guomindang government. Oppressive taxation, repeated famines, harsh political repression, and Chiang's reluctance to fight the Japanese alienated large segments of Chinese society during the 1930s.

wide section of the country, and their discipline and dedication — the Communists had been trained to pay a fair price for everything they were forced to take from the peasantry, to return all that was borrowed, to be courteous, to eschew looting and rape — were in sharp contrast to the rapaciousness and lawlessness often exhibited by the warlord and Guomindang soldiers. Most important, the leadership faction that emerged on the Long March — Mao, Zhou, Zhu, Lin Biao, Deng — would direct the Chinese Revolution for the next 50 years.

The Communists settled in Yanan. Most of Shaanxi is *loess* country. Loess is a yellowish-brown soil that geologists believe has been carried by easterly winds from Mongolia and deposited in Shaanxi and nearby provinces over the centuries. In Shaanxi the deposits have taken the form of strange configurations of hills, into which the inhabitants have built caves and dwellings. There were virtually no houses in Shaanxi in the 1930s; even the wealthiest inhabitants lived in the hillside caves, which were

At Yanan the Communists lived in caves carved into the hills and established a model of the type of society they wished to establish in China. Deng helped implement the Communists' land reform programs among the peasantry.

clean, comfortable, warm in the winter, and cool in the summer. Although the Communists may have been dismayed at their first glimpses of the seemingly forbidding landscape — "We didn't pick it," Mao told a visiting writer — the loess provided a deep topsoil that was extremely fertile, given adequate irrigation.

Yanan was the Communist capital from 1937 to 1947. The Communists put their theories into practice there and established a model of what they hoped could be achieved for China. Land was redistributed, and the peasants were encouraged to take part in cooperative ventures. Schools were established, with political education included as an important part of the curriculum. Egalitarianism was stressed, and the party's leaders lived as the cadres and peasants did, in sparely furnished caves. The oppressive taxation of the peasantry, which had continued under the Guomindang government (with an estimated 80 percent of the tax revenue earmarked for military expenditure), was eased. Visitors to Yanan were impressed with the contentment, dedication, and prosperity they found there. Western journalists and writers such as Edgar Snow and Agnes Smedley came to Yanan and wrote of the successful Communist experiment. Snow's book *Red Star over China* appeared in 1938, and as the first comprehensive Western account of the Communist struggle it was extremely influential in dispelling Chiang's assertions that the Communists were nothing more than "bandits." Snow's wife, Helen, wrote that the Communists were "a new people, creating a new world in the heart of the oldest and most changeless civilization on earth."

At the same time, Chiang's government was exposing its weaknesses. The Guomindang's support was chiefly urban based, coming mostly from the banking and business communities. Chiang was also supported by many intellectuals who hoped that he would provide China with the modern government that it so desperately needed. As Mao had astutely noted, however, the ultimate power lay in the support of the peasantry. ("The soldiers are fish, the people are the water" was one of the Red Army's mottoes.) Under the Guomindang, the peasants saw no change in their standard of living. The Guomindang's officials were notoriously corrupt, advertisements that Chiang's government did not embody the Confucian virtues. Famines in certain Chinese provinces in the middle and late 1930s further alienated the peasantry. Chiang outlawed all opposition to his government and employed secret police to ferret out dissidents, thousands of whom were shot. Chiang's authoritarian rule forced many of the intellectuals and liberals who were inclined to support him into the Communist camp.

The struggle with Japan brought these differences into sharper focus. Many Chinese were disenchanted by Chiang's refusal to challenge the Japanese in Manchuria. On December 9, 1935, 10,000 students in Beijing had demonstrated against the Japanese. Anti-Japanese societies were formed throughout China. Opposition was partic-

Newly mobilized university students train as soldiers in Guangzhou, 1938. Chiang was obsessed with a military solution to China's problems; he spent 80 percent of the taxes extracted from the peasantry on his army.

After their 1931 invasion of Manchuria (which they renamed Manchukuo), the Japanese installed Henry Pu-yi (center, with glasses) as their puppet ruler. The Communist policy of unyielding opposition to the Japanese presence won many supporters among patriotic Chinese.

ularly active in northern China, where the inhabitants were directly affected by the Japanese presence. After the initial invasion of Manchuria in 1931, the Japanese had moved into the province of Jehol. The entire area was then reconstituted as the state of Manchukuo, with Henry Pu-yi, who had been the child emperor at the time of the 1911 revolution, as Japan's puppet ruler. Since the establishment of Manchukuo the Japanese had been encroaching on other areas in northern China.

Almost immediately upon arrival in Shaanxi, Mao and the Communists had organized the peasants to resist the Japanese and had proposed to Chiang that a united front be established to fight the Japanese. Chiang refused. Zhou approached Manchuria's warlord, Zhang Xueliang, to enlist his support. Zhang's father, Zhang Zolin, had been the warlord of Manchuria until he was killed when a bomb planted by the Japanese demolished his train near Mukden in 1928. Nominally loyal to Chiang, Zhang Xueliang was tired of his appeasement of the Japanese.

Chiang went to the Shaanxi city of Xian in December 1936 to meet with Zhang. However, he was captured by Zhang's troops and held until he agreed to serve as leader of a united front. It is important to realize that although the Guomindang's support was ebbing and the Communists' was increasing, at that time only Chiang was capable of providing the semblance of a unified resistance to the Japanese. Zhou went to Xian to mediate between Zhang and Chiang and offered to put the Red Army under Chiang's command for purposes of fighting the Japanese. The Communist policy was a mixture of patriotism, pragmatism, and self-interest. Mao said at the time that "the war between China and Japan has furnished the best opportunity for the development of our party. Our policy is to devote seventy percent of our efforts to our own expansion, twenty percent to coping with the Guomindang, and only ten percent to fighting the Japanese." The Communists realized that Chiang and the Nationalists would bear the brunt of any fighting against the Japanese (though the Red Army had been rebuilt after the Long March, it still numbered only 80,000, while Chiang had 1.7 million men in uniform). With Chiang's release, an uneasy truce between the Communists and Nationalists went into effect. On July 7, 1937, a skirmish between Japanese and Chinese forces at the Marco Polo Bridge near Beijing led to widespread fighting and ultimately war between the two countries, setting the stage for Deng to demonstrate his military and tactical skills.

4

Crushing the Peanut

China's soldiers were not known for their fighting prowess, so the Japanese expected little difficulty in taking control of the nation. Beijing quickly fell. In the opinion of his aides Chiang's all-out defense of Shanghai was ill advised, but it illustrated to the Japanese that the Chinese could be more capable fighters than previously imagined. The battle for Shanghai lasted from August to November. The Japanese suffered 60,000 casualties; Chinese casualties were estimated to run in the hundreds of thousands. The Nationalists retreated, leaving their capital of Nanjing open to the invaders. In December 1937 the Japanese entered Nanjing and indulged in a riot of arson, looting, rape, torture, and murder. It is estimated that as many as 200,000 Chinese civilians were killed at Nanjing.

After Nanjing, Chiang retreated, content to trade "space for time." Chiang implemented a scorched-earth policy as he went, hoping to slow the Japanese advance by rendering the land unusable. He burned crops and blew up dikes, leaving the peasants starving and their land flooded. Chiang made his new capital at Chongqing, in southern Sichuan.

Chiang's strategy was predicated on his belief that it was inevitable that Japan's aggression in Asia would lead it into conflict with the Western powers, especially the United States. The United States had a long-standing interest in maintaining an "open door" in China, that is, ensuring that China re-

Some of our cadres have never come in close contact with the peasants. They isolate themselves from them. That is the landlord line.
—DENG XIAOPING stressing the importance of working with the peasants to his troops

A bewildered old man searches for his son among the new recruits called up to fight the Japanese. By 1940 Chiang had an army of nearly 2 million men, but his strategy was to avoid battle until the United States was forced to enter the war against Japan.

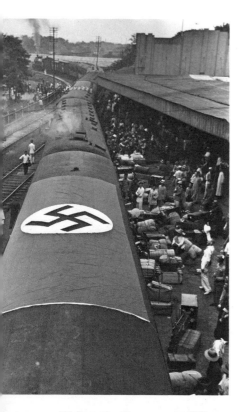

Chiang's German military advisers depart from his temporary capital at Hankow in 1938. German dictator Adolf Hitler was seeking an alliance with Japan and recalled the advisers after the outbreak of war between Japan and China.

mained open to all nations that wished to trade there. Possible Japanese hegemony in China threatened that policy. Public opinion in the United States was favorable toward China, which was seen as a nation moving toward democracy.

Chiang's strategy was also based on his conviction that China was unconquerable. During his studies of military history he had been much impressed by the French emperor Napoleon's failed invasion of Russia in 1812. The Russians retreated before Napoleon's superior forces, moving farther into the vast Russian heartland and destroying all that could have been of possible use to the French. Ultimately, the cold Russian climate, lack of food, and the country's size defeated the French.

Chiang believed that China's size and geography (virtually each of her provinces is protected by a natural geographic barrier, such as mountain ranges or rivers) made a similar strategy possible there, but his policy played into the Communists' hands. It was already felt that he was reluctant to fight the Japanese, and Communist propaganda painted his retreat as further evidence of his cowardice and lack of patriotism. The scorched-earth policy was harsh on the peasants, who were already less than enthusiastic about the Guomindang government, and Chiang's withdrawal to Chongqing left other areas of the country open to Communist organizational efforts. The Communists were identified with resistance to the Japanese, and by 1945 they claimed control over one-fifth of the nation.

In November 1937 the Japanese captured Taiyuan, the capital of Shanxi Province, and the Nationalists all but abandoned northern China. From the Yanan base the Eighth Route Army, as the Communist forces had been renamed, fought the Japanese, using the guerrilla tactics they had perfected.

In early 1938 Deng was made political commissar of the Eighth Route Army's 129th Division, then conducting guerrilla warfare in the mountains of Shanxi. The 129th Division was commanded by Liu Bocheng, known as the "One-eyed Dragon." Liu had opposed Mao during the anti–Luo Ming campaign but had been angered by the military blunders committed by the party at the outset of the Long March and had thrown his support to Mao at the Zunyi meeting. Thereafter Mao relied on Liu's military brilliance. For Deng the appointment was an opportune one. He remained in the position for the next 12 years, and the 129th Division became known as the Liu-Deng Army.

The 129th Division was based at Jin-Ji-Lu-Yu, on the border between Shaanxi, Shanxi, Sichuan, and Henan. The united front proved unworkable, and the Liu-Deng Army had to contend with warlords loyal to the Guomindang as well as the Japanese. The Liu-Deng Army participated in several major battles. The most important of these was the Hundred Regiments Offensive in the fall of 1940, in which Liu and Deng acted without Mao's prior consent in moving against Japanese communication lines in the Jin-Ji-Lu-Yu region. The success of the Hundred Regiments Offensive prompted the Japanese to direct action against northern China in the summer of 1941. One-quarter of the Communist forces and millions of civilians were killed, but the Japanese offensive seemed to confirm that the Communists were more concerned than the Nationalists with defending China.

Deng and Liu also carried on the Communists' work with the peasantry. Zhou noted that the peasants who joined the Eighth Route Army were often so poor that they did not bring their own chopsticks. Theodore White, an American journalist, observed the poverty of the peasants who fought the Japanese and wrote that they had been "born in the Middle Ages to die in the 20th century." Deng helped carry out the Communist land reform program. Soldiers worked with the peasants to cultivate new land, and grain production in the Communist areas was greatly boosted. Even Deng spent some time working the soil.

It was at about this time that Deng met and married his third wife, Zhuo Lin. Zhuo had been a student of physics at the University of Beijing when the Japanese occupied the city. Already a Communist convert, she traveled to Yanan to continue her studies at the Anti-Japanese and Political University, which the Communists had founded there. The marriage was by all accounts a happy one. Deng and Zhuo would eventually have five children.

By 1941 Japan believed that war with the United States was inevitable and on December 7, 1941, bombed the U.S. naval base at Pearl Harbor, Hawaii. The surprise raid was accompanied by Japanese attacks on the Philippines, Malaya, and Singapore. The United States immediately declared war on Japan, as well as on Germany and Italy, which were fighting Great Britain, France, and the Soviet Union. (Japan, Germany, and Italy were allied by virtue of the Tripartite Pact of September 1940; together these nations were known as the Axis powers, and the United States, Soviet Union, France, and Great Britain were referred to as the Allies.)

It was important to the U.S. war effort that China put up a stiff resistance to the Japanese. Money and weapons were made available to Chiang, who was still seen as the only man capable of uniting China. Chiang was made supreme commander of the China-Burma-India theater of war, with U.S. general Joseph Stilwell as his chief of staff.

At that point Chiang was interested more in diplomacy than he was in fighting. After Chiang had retreated to Chongqing, the Japanese had essentially foregone any further offensives and consolidated their hold over eastern China (except for the Communist-controlled areas in the north), preferring to prepare for the oncoming war in the Pacific. Once World War II began, Chiang was hopeful that he could get his new allies to do much of the fighting while he preserved his troops for the battle with the Communists. According to Chiang, the Communists still presented the greatest danger to China. "The Japanese," he said, "are a disease of the skin. The Communists are a disease of the heart." In 1942, with the war at something of a standstill, Mao launched a "rectification" campaign designed to consolidate his grip on the party and eliminate the continued influence of the 28 Bolsheviks and other critics. Mao believed the most important basis for a revolution was the proper attitude and ideology among party members and troops, and he was increasingly confident of the correctness of his own policies. No longer would the Chinese Communists look to the Soviet Union for leadership. While the Soviet example had been useful, Mao believed that communism in China would develop in its own way, according to China's own historical conditions. The goal of the rectification campaign was to create ideological solidarity within the CCP. Deng returned to Yanan to take part in it and then helped to spread the reforms to his own area. Zhou Enlai later reported that Deng had "sincerely cooperated" with the movement, which lasted until 1944, and that the party had been satisfied with his achievements.

In November 1943 Chiang met with President Franklin Roosevelt of the United States and Prime Minister Winston Churchill of Great Britain in Cairo, Egypt. Chiang was delighted at this confirmation of his status as one of the Allied "Big Four" (the absent Soviet leader, Joseph Stalin, being the other) and took further pride in Roosevelt's agreement to arm and train 90 Guomindang divisions and mount a major offensive in Burma, where the Japanese had closed the Burma Road, a crucial supply line.

Despite Stilwell's prodding, Chiang would not launch an attack on the Japanese. The American general had spent many years in China, spoke the language, and believed he understood the Chinese

Chiang receives the Medal of the Legion of Merit from chief of staff Joseph Stilwell in 1943. Appalled at the corruption of the Guomindang government and Chiang's unwillingness to fight, Stilwell and his advisers recommended that the United States give aid to the Communists and incorporate them into the regular Chinese forces.

people, but he had disliked Chiang from the outset. In his dispatches to Washington he contemptuously referred to Chiang as "Peanut" and the "little rattlesnake." He found Chiang guileful and duplicitous, and Chiang disliked Stilwell's bluntness. Stilwell also bore the brunt of Chiang's resentment of the conditions under which American aid was granted. The United States' other allies were free to distribute the money as they saw fit, but Chiang needed Stilwell's approval for his expenditures.

Stilwell found Chiang's fighting forces inept, and he believed the Guomindang government corrupt and inefficient. U.S. military observers and foreign service officers had been making their way to Yanan and were impressed by what they found there. The Communist troops were well organized and ready for battle; Mao's followers were communists but were more flexible than their Soviet counterparts and could just as easily be thought of as agrarian democrats. Evans Carlson, an American officer, was tremendously impressed with Deng, whom he described as "short, chunky and physically tough," with a "mind as keen as mustard" and an excellent grasp of international affairs.

The Japanese attack on the United States had been based on the belief that the United States would be unwilling to fight a prolonged war in the Pacific, particularly once it became involved against Nazi Germany in Europe, and would eventually negotiate a peace that would allow Japan to keep part of its Asian empire. The Japanese military gained territory in the Pacific until it was defeated by U.S. forces at the Battle of Midway in the spring of 1942. Thereafter the U.S. forces fought their way slowly across the Pacific, and by the summer of 1944 U.S. bombers were devastating the Japanese home islands. In central and southern China the Japanese unleashed a massive offensive that caught the Guomindang forces completely unprepared. Chiang had sent several of his best divisions to Burma (the promised Allied operation there and the 90 U.S.-trained divisions had never materialized), and his remaining troops were routed. Over 700,000 of Chiang's troops were killed or wounded.

Banners in Shanghai in 1945 proclaim China's joy at Japan's defeat in World War II, but the Communists and Nationalists resumed their civil war soon afterward.

This was the last straw for Stilwell, who had been impressed by the reports from Yanan. "The cure for China's trouble is the elimination of Chiang Kai-shek," he wrote in the journal he kept at the time. Stilwell wrote that Chiang "can't see that the mass of Chinese people welcome the Reds [the Communists] as being the only visible hope of relief from the crushing taxation and the abuses of the army." Stilwell urged Roosevelt to put him in command of the U.S. and Chinese forces and to incorporate the Communists into the main body of the Chinese army. Roosevelt initially concurred, but Chiang refused, and the stalemate was resolved by Stilwell's being relieved of his position.

Japan surrendered to the Allies on August 14, 1945, shortly after U.S. atomic bombs obliterated Hiroshima and Nagasaki. U.S. mediators arranged a meeting between Chiang and Mao Zedong in Chongqing in late August, but no agreement could be reached. Within weeks of the end of World War II the Chinese civil war had resumed.

By July 1946 the Nationalists had launched an all-out offensive against the Communists, whom they outnumbered four to one. The Nationalists had acquired modern military technology from the

When the civil war resumed after World War II the Nationalist forces outnumbered the Red Army by a ratio of four to one. These soldiers of the Communist New Fourth Army are well armed, but many lack shoes appropriate for use in combat.

United States during World War II and confiscated additional arms from the defeated Japanese. Funds given Chiang by the United States to help China rebuild were funneled into the military budget, and the Nationalists won a number of early victories.

After 1945 the Communist army was reorganized and renamed the People's Liberation Army (PLA). Deng remained political commissar of the 129th Division, now called the 2nd Field Army. It was the PLA's largest division, still under the command of Liu Bocheng, and it was feared by the Guomindang.

In March 1947 Mao instructed the 2nd Field Army to move southward, in order to lure Guomindang troops away from Yanan. With 50,000 troops, Liu and Deng crossed the Huang He (Yellow River) into Guomindang territory in Shandong Province. There Deng displayed what one cadre described as his usual "sincere, calm" manner. At a meeting in a schoolhouse, Deng told his men: "Revolution is a difficult thing. If you want to make revolution, you shouldn't be afraid of difficulties. If you are afraid of difficulties, don't make revolution."

The Liu-Deng Army then moved at a breakneck pace — 30 miles a day — across the central China plain toward the base of the Fourth Front Army in the Dabie Mountains near Nanjing. Unable to see the broader Communist strategy, the Guomindang believed the Communist troops were fleeing.

One of the earliest photos of Deng (left), with commander Liu Bocheng (with glasses) and Zhang Jichun in the headquarters of the Second Field Army in 1949. The Liu-Deng Army, as it came to be known, was instrumental in the Communist defeat of Chiang and the Nationalists.

In March 1949 Deng (second from right) attended the session of the CCP's Central Committee where "Mao Zedong Thought" was officially adopted as the guiding principle for all party work. After the Communists took power Mao rewarded Deng's loyalty by appointing him to several important government positions.

Chiang's army was demoralized, impoverished, and crippled by corruption within the Guomindang government. Theodore White and Annalee Jacoby wrote that at the end of World War II the Guomindang army was "a pulp, a tired, dispirited, unorganized mass, despised by the enemy, alien to its own people, neglected by its government, ridiculed by its allies." Two years of defeats by the Communists had not improved its morale. Its best troops were concentrated in the north, and in Manchuria the Nationalists had lost 150,000 men to an army led by the Communist general Lin Biao.

The Liu-Deng Army quickly set up base in the Dabie Mountains, in terrain well suited to guerrilla warfare. Deng was appointed first secretary of the Central China Bureau, which was to carry out agricultural reforms and conduct military operations against the Guomindang in the central China plain. As elsewhere, the land reform program consisted of appropriating property from rich landlords and redistributing it among the peasants. Deng urged his cadres to get close to the peasants and warned them, "If you look down on the peasants you will also be looked down on."

By September 1948 the Communist army was able to take the offensive. The 2nd Field Army now numbered 250,000 men and was reorganized into the Central Plain Army, which joined forces with another field army, under Chen Yi, and engaged the Guomindang troops in a fierce battle in the Huai River area. In one of the most important battles of the civil war, 550,000 Communist troops fought in rain, sleet, and snow for 2 months before defeating

Communist soldiers await orders in Shanghai, 1949. Mao had expressly forbidden looting or pillaging, and the Chinese people found the well-disciplined Communists a welcome contrast to the rapacious Nationalist troops.

On October 1, 1949, on a simple platform in Beijing's Forbidden City, the former residence of the emperors, Mao proclaimed the establishment of the People's Republic of China.

the Nationalists. The Nationalists suffered casualties of over 200,000. The Huai-Hai campaign (named for the Huai River and the nearby Lunghai Railway) was one of the greatest battles in modern history and made possible the Communist liberation of the central Chinese cities of Wuhan and Nanjing. Beijing fell to Lin Biao's army shortly after. Chiang's government and army fled to the south. On October 1, 1949, at the Gate of Heavenly Peace in Beijing's Forbidden City, the former residence of the emperors, Mao proclaimed the establishment of the People's Republic of China. Beijing, the ancient imperial capital, was made the new capital. Two months later Chiang left the mainland to the Communists and took his government to the island of Taiwan.

5

Emperor of the Southwest

The long years of war had left Deng an experienced and capable leader who had earned the epithet "always correct" from his comrades. He was given three top posts within the new government. He was appointed to the new legislature — the Political Consultation Conference — and made council member of the Central People's Government and People's Revolutionary Military Councils. His first task was in the south of China, where he was sent to help chase the remnants of the Guomindang from their last remaining strongholds.

After the Nationalists fled to Taiwan, Deng became mayor of their former capital of Chongqing. It was a city he knew well from his days at preparatory school. His new titles of first secretary and political commissar for the southwest made him the most powerful man in the region, dubbed by his detractors the "emperor of the southwest."

The southwest had remained under Guomindang control throughout the war, and its people had had little contact with the Communists. It was Deng's job to bring land reform to the region. Much of the Chinese populace was receptive, even euphoric, about the Communist victory. A long period of war

Veteran revolutionaries only end up as monsters and ghosts.
—DENG XIAOPING

Mao tips his cap to supporters in Beijing, which the Communists made China's capital. The foremost problem the new government faced was raising the standard of living of the peasantry.

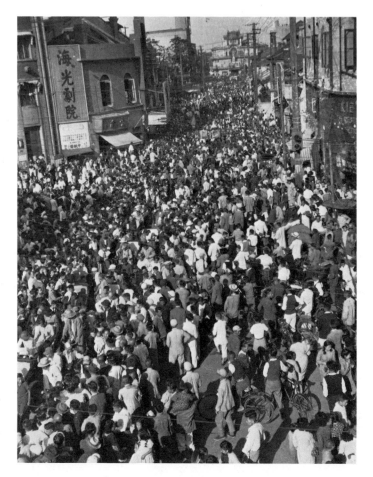

Hordes of people thronged the streets of Shanghai to celebrate the birth of the People's Republic in October 1949. The widespread support the Communists enjoyed among the populace was the single most crucial element in their victory.

had finally ended. The Chinese were eager to have peace and order returned to their lives and willing to cooperate with the CCP to achieve that goal. Noted China scholar John King Fairbank wrote of the establishment of the Communist government: "Here was a conquering army of country boys who were strictly self-disciplined, polite and helpful, at the opposite pole from the looting and raping warlord troops and even the departing Nationalists. Here was a dedicated government that really cleaned things up — not only the drains and the streets, but also all the beggars, prostitutes and petty criminals, all of whom were rounded up for reconditioning. Here was a new China one could be proud of."

But it was a new China faced with overwhelming

difficulties, both at home and abroad. Soaring inflation, inadequate industrial and food production, and chaotic local administration were the legacy of the long years of war. The crippled economy had to be revived, and the ancient system that gave landlords dominion over most of the country's soil had to be abolished.

The land reform campaign began in earnest in 1950. The new government defined the Chinese people as being composed of four classes — the proletariat, peasantry, petty bourgeoisie, and national bourgeoisie. The peasantry was subdivided into landlord, rich peasant, middle peasant, poor peasant, or farm laborer. The Communists intended to turn the class system upside down. In the social upheaval of the early years of the People's Republic it was best to belong to the lowest possible class. Women, who were not allowed to own property in the old China, now received that right.

The land reform campaign was completed in two short years but not without violence. Accusation meetings at which peasants criticized landlords and other peasants richer than themselves were held. The luckiest landlords escaped with clipped fingernails (long fingernails were a sign that one belonged to the gentry or another nonlaboring class) and were given small plots of land to farm. After five years of farming their landlord status could be removed if it was decided that they had been truly reformed. Harsher measures were more frequent, and many landlords and former members of the gentry were executed. Several million people were killed during the first years of land reform.

The Communists succeeded in carrying out other economic reforms. Much of the wartime inflation was curbed, and a centralized banking system and uniform currency were established, making possible coordinated economic planning. Three fruitful harvests (1950–52) helped ease the food shortage, and by 1952 the previous peaks of production in pig iron, cement, steel, oil, coal, electricity, and flour had been surpassed. The nation's railway and highway systems were expanded.

Trade union members in Shanghai enact the arrest of a Guomindang agent during the 1950 celebration of the 22nd anniversary of the creation of the Red Army. The end of the civil war and optimism for the new government created a general sense of euphoria in China.

It took only a year for China's new government to demonstrate that it would play an active role in foreign affairs if it felt the nation's interests were involved. Late in October 1950, 200,000 Chinese troops joined the forces of its communist neighbor, North Korea, in its war with U.S. and United Nations' forces defending South Korea. Three years of bloody fighting resulted in little gain for either side and left Korea still divided. The damage to the Korean nation was enormous and costly. More than 2.5 million South Koreans were left homeless by the war; 1 million civilians lost their lives. The Chinese military suffered 1 million casualties and demonstrated that it was technologically inadequate and unready for modern warfare, despite its success in the civil war.

In Deng's region in the southwest, as in the rest of China, the Korean War forced an acceleration in the agrarian and political reform movements. The slogan "Resist America, Aid Korea" was used to arouse the Chinese people's nationalism, and the

Sampans crowd the docks in Shanghai. China's huge population and crowded cities made the task of modernizing more difficult, but Mao believed China's manpower could also be a valuable resource whose energy could be tapped to hasten industrialization as well as collectivization.

war became an excuse for a more rigid control over the Chinese people. A program aimed at eliminating counterrevolutionaries — broadly defined as those who opposed the revolution and often, in effect, anyone who opposed government policy — was instituted, as were nationwide campaigns against corruption, wastefulness, and crimes against the state. Mao himself admitted that 700,000 Chinese were executed during the campaign against counterrevolutionaries, and other people estimate that the final count was even higher. The anticorruption campaigns were directed primarily at the government bureaucrats and administrators held over from the Guomindang era and middle-class businessmen and merchants.

By the time the CCP came to power its leading figures had worked together for many years. Those who had led the Communists through the early years of struggle with the Nationalists, the Long March, the Yanan years, the war with the Japanese,

Beijing workers carried hundreds of portraits of Mao at the first anniversary of the People's Republic in 1950. His face had become the symbol of the revolution, and statues and huge murals of the leader were commissioned throughout China.

Deng (second from left) with Liu Bocheng (center) and other leaders of the revolution. Having demonstrated his political and military skills, Deng was appointed to top posts in the new government and made responsible for enacting party policy in southwest China.

and then the civil war were those who wielded the most power in China's new government. In the early years of the new state Mao had sent his ablest men to the regions of China where they were needed most, but as the situation in China's provinces stabilized, he recalled many of his favorites to Beijing.

In 1952 Deng was transferred to Beijing and made one of five vice-premiers of the state administrative council, which was similar to a presidential cabinet. A few months later he was 1 of 15 members appointed to the new state planning committee, which was to draw up and direct China's first Five-Year Plan. The Five-Year Plan was derived from the Soviet Union's similar program, in which all elements of the economy were planned out and directed by the government. Production goals and quotas were established for virtually all of the nation's industries.

China's first Five-Year Plan began in January 1953 and was characterized by an emphasis on industrial, rather than agricultural, production. Steel production was to be quadrupled, electric power output doubled, cement production doubled, and the manufacture of machine tools tripled. In the countryside the implementation of the Five-Year Plan was marked by increased collectivization. Private ownership of land was discouraged, and cooperative farms and communes were introduced. The earlier land reform programs had redistributed land to the peasantry, but private ownership had been maintained. Mao saw this as merely the first step toward collectivization, whereby land would be owned in common. By 1956 more than 90 percent of the peasantry lived on upward of 2 million agricultural cooperatives of 50 families or more.

The Chinese Communists had mixed emotions about the leader of the Soviet Union, Joseph Stalin.

The Nationalists launched numerous and sporadic raids on the Chinese mainland from the island of Taiwan (Formosa), where Chiang had taken the Guomindang government after his defeat by the Communists. In 1951 Nationalist bombers destroyed homes in Shanghai.

Peasants wait to receive their newly apportioned lots after the implementation of the Communists' land reform programs, which took land from the landlords and gave it to the peasants. Several million landlords were denounced as class enemies and executed.

With the success of their revolution the Chinese Communists had grown increasingly confident and independent. They suspected that Stalin wanted to run their affairs, and they remembered that it was Stalin who had urged cooperation with the Nationalists. Mao was also steadfast in insisting that the revolution in China could not mimic the Soviet model but had to develop according to China's unique history. For his part, Stalin resented the independence of the Chinese and their willingness to diverge from communist dogma. He seemed to regard Mao as something of a rude and unlettered peasant, incapable of understanding fundamental Marxist doctrine, and wondered whether the Chinese were communists at all. At one point he likened the Chinese Communists to radishes because both were red on the outside, white on the inside.

Despite their differences, Mao realized that China could not modernize quickly without the aid of the Soviet Union. Mao had once indicated that he thought the United States was the most suitable country to help China's postwar economic development, but after World War II the alliance between the United States and the Soviet Union broke down, and anticommunism became the cornerstone of U.S. foreign policy. China had neither the financing nor the skilled personnel needed for industrialization and turned for assistance to the Soviet Union, which provided loans and technical assistance in exchange for Chinese agricultural products and minerals. The Soviets and Chinese also reached agreement on a program that enabled 6,500 Chinese students to study in the Soviet Union, and the Soviet Union provided China with extensive military aid.

The early years of the People's Republic were a rewarding period for Deng. The country was at peace, and the first Five-Year Plan was a success. Deng was made minister of finance in 1953 and quickly demonstrated that he was as adept at economic planning as he had been at political indoctrination and military tactics. The new finance minister watched with pleasure as his countrymen's standard of living improved measurably. China was still poor, but good harvests and increased industrial output gave reason for optimism. Happily married, in good health, and politically well connected, Deng must have viewed with pride the early success of the Communist revolution he had helped to make.

In retrospect, Deng enjoyed the most peaceful and satisfying part of his political career during the years 1950 to 1956; the revolution was accomplished, national construction was in progress and China's international position was acknowledged.
—CHING LEE
author

6

Breaking with the Soviets

The Soviet Union proved to be a difficult ally, willing to help China only on terms favorable to itself. Mao had made his first trip outside China in December 1949 when he went to Moscow to meet with Stalin. He found the Soviet leader less than cordial. Stalin kept Mao waiting for days at a time before meeting with him and was a tough and unyielding negotiator. Ross Terrill, one of Mao's biographers, said that "Stalin saw socialist China as a new pupil to be given a place in his Marxist class, alongside Poland and Hungary and the others [Eastern European countries that had become Soviet satellites after World War II]. He expected new China to honor — and supply goods to — the Soviet fatherland just as East Europe did." To obtain the economic assistance he needed from the Soviet Union, Mao had to agree to the independence of Outer Mongolia, Soviet access to railway lines in eastern China, and a shared use of the mineral resources in the western regions.

The Manchurian leader Gao Gang began developing a separate, more amicable relationship with Stalin. Stalin was interested in Manchuria because it

> *Both superpowers [the United States and the Soviet Union] subject other countries to subversion and aggression and exploit them economically.*
> —DENG XIAOPING

Deng, then secretary general of the CCP, with Premier Zhou Enlai (left) and Politburo member and Beijing mayor Peng Chen (right). He had recently returned from the 20th Conference of the Communist party in Moscow, held in February 1956, where Soviet leader Nikita Khrushchev denounced the excesses of his predecessor, Joseph Stalin.

By the late 1950s, Mao (third from right) and Deng (far left) disagreed on the best way to develop China's economy. Mao also suspected that some CCP leaders, including Zhou (third from left), resented his power. Zhu De (fourth from right) was dismayed at the dissension among the longtime revolutionary comrades.

was the most heavily industrialized section of China and contained railway links with the Soviet Union. Stalin and Gao concluded their own trade agreement. Although Gao's independence rankled Mao, he was reluctant to act directly against the Manchurian because of Gao's friendliness with Stalin. When Mao began consolidating the central government, he asked Gao to come to Beijing to serve as chairman of the state planning committee. In Beijing Gao allied himself with another recent arrival from eastern China, Rao Shushi, but when Stalin died in 1953 Mao moved against both men. He placed the trustworthy Deng in charge of the purge. In veiled language, a resolution was introduced that accused some party members of treating their areas of responsibility as "independent kingdoms." Gao and Rao were removed from their positions, arrested, interrogated, and expelled from the party. The official version held that Gao committed suicide, but some people, Stalin's successor Nikita Khrushchev among them, charged that he was executed. His suicide did not satisfy the party. Deng introduced a final resolution charging that Gao had "attempted to make an independent kingdom of Manchuria" and had "not only refused to bow to the Party and admit his guilt, but even made his last expression of rebellion against the Party by killing himself."

Deng's loyalty to Mao was repaid with promotions within the party hierarchy. He was made secretary general of the CCP in 1954 and was elected to the politburo the following year. He began playing host to foreign visitors and taking a role in forming China's foreign policy. In February 1956 he traveled to Moscow to attend the 20th Congress of the Communist Party of the Soviet Union as part of a delegation led by Zhu De. At the congress Khrushchev made an early, public speech in which he declared that war between communism and capitalism was not necessarily inevitable. While this represented a daring departure from orthodox Marxism, Khrushchev's later, secret speech — so called because it was intended to be heard only by the delegates — was even more shocking. Khrushchev denounced Stalin as paranoid and possessed of a "sickly suspicion" and as a man who used his "unlimited power" to "choke . . . a person morally and physically." Stalin had been responsible for the arrest, imprisonment, and execution of innocent Soviet citizens, Khrushchev said (historians have estimated the number of Soviet citizens imprisoned during Stalin's purges in the millions), and it was his incompetence and the unreadiness of the military due to his purges of officers that led to the Soviet Union's

Deng watches Mao sign a declaration at a conference of communist nations in Moscow in 1957. Although by this time he disagreed with Deng on many important issues, Mao praised Deng to his Soviet hosts as one of his government's most able men.

The Great Leap Forward of the late 1950s was Mao's attempt to industrialize China's economy through widespread collectivization of its manpower. Poor planning, mismanagement, inadequate technology, and popular unrest, however, ensured its failure.

suffering at the hands of Nazi Germany during World War II, when Soviet casualties (both civilian and military) numbered nearly 20 million. Khrushchev condemned the cult of the individual that had risen around Stalin and the way that Stalin had concentrated absolute power in his own hands.

Deng was deeply impressed by what he heard in Moscow. Upon his return to Beijing he was placed in charge of the agenda for the Eighth Party Congress of the CCP. Some of the party leaders, including Liu Shaoqi and Mao's Jinggangshan comrade Peng Dehuai, had become disillusioned with Mao's leadership, in part because of the failure of the agricultural collectivization program, which had been resisted by the peasants and had resulted in small harvests, food shortages, and famine, and in part because of what they saw as Mao's increasingly dictatorial rule. It had become customary to preface speeches with laudatory references to Mao, and the 1945 party constitution had fixed "Mao Zedong Thought" as the guide for all communists. That same constitution gave Mao virtual supreme authority over the party and government by making him chairman of the party Central Committee, politburo, and secretariat. (The politburo and Central Committee were the party's primary decision-making organs, and the secretariat oversaw the party's day-to-day operations.)

At the Eighth Party Congress, Liu criticized Mao for acting arbitrarily and extolling himself at the expense of the party. Deng, who at the behest of the party had replaced Mao as head of the secretariat, offered even harsher judgments. Party leaders should stand within the party, not above it, Deng said. Using Stalin as an example, Deng stated that "serious consequences can follow from the deification of the individuals" because "no individuals are free from flaws and mistakes in their activities." Deng's assertion that "loyalty to a leader is essentially a matter of showing attachment to the interests of the party, to the interests of the class, to the interests of the people, and not of making a myth out of the individual concerned" was echoed in an amendment to the party constitution that eliminated the reference to Mao Zedong Thought and maintained that the party was "the vanguard of the Chinese working class, the highest form of its class organization." At the same time, Deng still professed loyalty to Mao, noting that "Marxism never denies the importance of the individual's role in history" and that Mao himself had warned the party to beware of the cult of personality.

Although Mao disapproved of the de-Stalinization campaign in the Soviet Union — "Stalin's mistakes amounted to only 30 percent of the whole and his achievements to 70 percent" — he was always aware of which way the wind was blowing. Initially he embraced the trend toward liberalization by asking China's intellectuals to freely voice their criticism of the government. They should "let a hundred flowers bloom, let a hundred schools of thought contend." The intellectuals and students responded with a barrage of critical comment and suggestion, and Mao brought the Hundred Flowers Campaign to an end within a month, labeling the criticisms "poisonous weeds" that had to be uprooted. An ag-

> *Some people tend to criticize others in order to achieve fame, stamping on others' shoulders to move up to key positions.*
> —DENG XIAOPING

gressive antirightist purge was directed at those who had spoken out. Though Mao was unhappy with the harshness of the response to the Hundred Flowers Campaign, it accomplished exactly what Mao had intended. The campaign enabled Mao to identify dissident elements within society, and because the criticism it unleashed was directed mainly at the party, not him, it enabled Mao to claim the loyalty of the masses and purge those within the party who sought to undermine him. Those who had agreed with the campaign and the criticisms were denounced as rightists, while others could be attacked as being out of touch with the masses.

Despite his growing independence and power, Deng remained in Mao's favor. In his speech to the Eighth Party Congress Deng had emphasized that "the basis of the Party is a unified ideology." In a speech made in September of the same year, Deng accused the intellectuals of trying to "restore capitalism and reactionary rule." He added that "the leadership of the CCP, the principles of the proletariat dictatorship and democratic centralism should never be questioned."

In October 1957 Deng traveled with Mao to Moscow to attend a summit meeting of the leaders of the communist countries. The two men were on very friendly terms. In Moscow Mao told Khrushchev that he had little admiration for Liu Shaoqi, Zhou Enlai, or Zhu De, but he was enthusiastic about Deng. "See that little man over there?" he asked Khrushchev. "He's highly intelligent and has a great future ahead of him."

The gulf between the two largest communist countries was broadening. Mao believed that the Soviet Union had grown cautious and was no longer committed to the worldwide communist revolution. Just prior to the conference, the Soviet Union had launched Sputnik I, the world's first artificial satellite. Mao saw this as a sign of the superiority of the communist bloc and proclaimed "the east wind prevails over the west wind." Khrushchev was more cautious. With nuclear weapons, he explained, conventional technological and military superiority, the

Some people say this was a covert scheme. We say it was an overt one. For we made it plain to the enemy beforehand: only when ghosts and monsters are allowed to come into the open can they be wiped out; only when poisonous weeds are allowed to sprout from the soil can they be uprooted.

—MAO ZEDONG
revolutionary and leader of China from 1949 to 1976, on the Hundred Flowers Campaign

size of armies, even the revolutionary fervor that had carried the communists to power, could be rendered meaningless. It was a time for realism and negotiation. Mao scoffed. People, not weapons, made war and revolution. Khrushchev had fallen for American propaganda. The atom bomb was a "paper tiger." Besides, Mao told Khrushchev, nuclear war would not matter to the Soviet Union or China. The people in their two countries, he jested, were so sexually active that their populations would quickly be replenished. Khrushchev did not find the remark funny and thought Mao irresponsible, if not irrational.

The Chinese and Soviets also disagreed on the topic of domestic policy. Mao had grown impatient with the progress made under the Five-Year Plan. Two weeks after returning from Moscow he announced the Great Leap Forward, which would utilize China's greatest resource, its manpower, to further industrial and agricultural expansion and enable China to "overtake Britain in 15 years."

The Chinese people were urged to be both "red and expert." Industrial expansion was to be achieved without urbanization. Increased steel production was targeted as an important goal. Peasants were encouraged to build steel furnaces on their

During the Great Leap Forward most of the peasantry was organized into large communes. All property was collectively owned, and schooling, health care, and other services were provided by the commune. These Chinese are watching television at a commune in Yanan.

land, into which they poured their kitchen utensils and even the hinges from their doors to be melted down to make steel. Unfortunately many backyard industrialists were more "red" than "expert". The steel produced in their furnaces was of low quality.

In the countryside Mao introduced the idea of the peoples' communes, which he believed would be the quickest route to socialist agriculture. By November 98 percent of the farming population lived on communes — large cooperative units of about 25,000 people. Families lived together in houses owned by the state. They worked state-owned property and dined in communal halls. Their children were taken care of in schools and child-care centers run by the state. Throughout the countryside there was a flurry of activity. French visitors to China remarked that the busy Chinese in their functional monochrome clothing looked like "blue ants."

The Great Leap Forward demanded that the people put in long hours for meager rewards. Discontent was widespread and was reflected in the actual economic and agricultural output. Party leaders with little knowledge of agriculture supervised the farming on the communes with disastrous results. A foolish campaign against sparrows, which eat grain, was launched. Only after sparrows had been almost eliminated was it noticed that the birds eat insects that are equally damaging to crops. A plague of insects swarmed across China's fields.

The peasants were bitter that the party that had come to power shouting the slogan "land to the tiller" had taken back what it had so recently given. In the early years of the Soviet Union, Lenin did not organize the peasants into communes because he recognized that "it is essential to wake up the activity of the small farmer, to give him an incentive, to stimulate his work." The poor planning in China led to disaster. Production in most industrial sectors plummeted, and the agricultural economy was wrecked. Food shortages plagued China well into the 1960s.

Deng was apparently of two minds about the Great Leap Forward. He supported it at the outset

He [Deng] perceived the disaster of the Great Leap Forward and spoke his mind. He was not one of those who came to Lushan Mountain with two speeches in his pockets, one to use if Peng Dehuai prevailed, one to use if Mao won out.
—HARRISON E. SALISBURY
American historian

but came to believe that Mao had unrealistic expectations of rapid progress. "A donkey is certainly slow," he quipped, "but at least it rarely has an accident." Many years later he admitted that he and other high-ranking political cadres shared the blame for its failure.

In 1959 Mao admitted that the Great Leap Forward had been a mistake. In a surprising move he resigned from his position as head of state, although he retained the CCP chairmanship. It is not certain whether this was an uncharacteristic act of contrition or whether he was pressured into it by his colleagues. Liu Shaoqi became China's new head of state.

At a conference in Lushan in July 1959 Peng Dehuai, now defense minister, boldly criticized Mao for the failure of the Great Leap Forward. Peng was also upset about the deterioration of relations with the Soviet Union, which had continued when Khrushchev, perhaps influenced by Mao's inflammatory remarks on nuclear warfare, had reneged on a promise to provide China with technology that would enable it to build its own nuclear weapons. At the conference Peng called the Great Leap For-

Liberation Theater actors stage a farcical attack on the imperial dynasty. Under the watchful eye of Mao's wife Jiang Qing, only those theatrical works that contributed to the people's understanding of class struggle and Communist ideology were allowed to be staged.

In the summer of 1963 Deng (fourth from left) headed a delegation to Moscow that was charged with repairing China's deteriorating relations with the Soviet Union. The most important Chinese leaders, including Zhou (front, third from right), Liu Shaoqi (to left of Deng), and Mao (right of Deng) greeted him at the Beijing airport on his arrival home.

ward "hasty and excessive." Mao was shocked at the blunt criticism. Still able to muster sufficient support to carry out his wishes, he had Peng replaced as defense minister by Lin Biao. As Zhu De watched the argument between the former colleagues he realized that the revolutionary camaraderie and spirit of Yanan and the early years was gone forever. "And to think we all ate out of the same dish in the past," he exclaimed.

At Lushan Mao did admit that mistakes had been made in implementing the Great Leap Forward. Liu and Deng assumed increased responsibilities and were able to apply their own ideas to China's economy. Deng's strategies were similar to those used by Lenin in introducing his New Economic Policy in the Soviet Union nearly 40 years earlier. Deng believed that a degree of capitalism could be allowed within a socialist economy. Such common features of capitalist societies as private ownership of small plots and material incentives could be used to spur China's economy, which was in drastic need of repair. Even the political radicals were willing to tread Deng and Liu's "capitalist road" for the time being.

In 1961 Deng went to the countryside in Hebei Province to study the economic situation. Based on his findings, Deng helped put together the "Sixty Articles on Agriculture," which reorganized China's farming communities. The largest communes were divided into smaller cooperative units. Peasants were given the right to own small plots, and free markets appeared in the countryside again. Similar approaches were used in other parts of China. Deng believed that a policy should be judged on its effectiveness rather than on whether it adhered to Marxist doctrine. "Whatever style the masses want, adopt that style. What may be illegal, make it legal," he said. In the most famous expression of his pragmatic approach, Deng said, "So long as it raises output, private farming is permissible. White or black, so long as cats can catch mice they are good cats."

Deng's theories left him at odds with Mao. Deng believed that many of the intellectuals who had been purged during the antirightist campaign should be rehabilitated, while Mao was not inclined toward leniency. Mao believed that ideological education and political indoctrination were more important than traditional education, but Deng thought being "expert" was more important than being "red," particularly if China was to catch up with the more developed Western nations. Deng loved traditional Chinese opera and hated the new revolutionary operas that were designed to illustrate political themes. The new operas were sponsored by Mao's wife, Jiang Qing, a former actress who was becoming increasingly active in politics. Deng was not afraid to oppose her and insisted, "He who does not know the Sichuan opera knows nothing of civilization." Mao was beginning to see Deng and Liu as insubordinate. Deng and others within the CCP continued to act independently of Mao, who resented his reduced role and complained that he was being treated like a "dead ancestor."

Mao and Deng continued to agree on foreign policy. Conditions during the "three bitter years" following the Great Leap Forward were worsened by the widening rift between the Soviet Union and China. Khrushchev accused Mao of being "like Sta-

Deng ran domestic policy with scant regard for Mao's views. [His] motto was "take reality as your starting point," and his version of reality contrasted strikingly with the utopian view of China propagated abroad by self-proclaimed friends of China.
—ROGER GARSIDE
British diplomat and historian, on Deng's differences with Mao

Party luminaries and massive crowds feted Deng on his return from Moscow in 1963, but his mission had been unsuccessful. The tenuous alliance between the Soviet Union and China had been severed, a casualty of what Mao perceived as the Soviet Union's growing conservatism.

lin . . . of spinning theories detached from the realities of the modern world." With his belief that communism could peacefully overtake capitalism, Khrushchev, said the Chinese, was "emasculating, betraying, and revising" Marxism-Leninism. In 1958 the Soviet Union refused to help the Chinese with a plan to capture the Nationalist-controlled islands of Quemoy and Matsu and tried to discourage the scheme. The following year Khrushchev praised U.S. president Dwight Eisenhower as a seeker of peace, and Mao worried that the United States and Soviet Union might someday form an alliance against China.

In July 1960 the Soviet Union abruptly informed China that it was recalling all its experts and advisers. Some Soviet technicians brought the blueprints for unfinished factories and projects with them back to Moscow. In November Deng and Liu went to Moscow to attend a summit conference of the world's communist nations.

The split between the world's two most important communist countries had begun to affect the world communist movement. Many communist parties in the developing nations of Africa and Asia now looked to Mao and the Chinese as the most likely supporters of revolution, and Khrushchev resented the CCP's newfound prestige. It was hoped that the Moscow conference would help settle the dispute. Deng was given his most important diplomatic responsibility to that point, as China's chief spokesman at the conference. Even though Deng handled his task adeptly, the differences between China and the Soviet Union remained unresolved.

The situation continued to deteriorate. In 1962 China denounced the Soviet Union for its capitulation to the United States after it agreed to remove missiles it had installed in Cuba. There were repeated confrontations between the two nations over long-standing border disputes. When Khrushchev sided with India during a brief Chinese-Indian border clash, the Chinese openly insulted the Soviet leader. Soviet youths smashed the windows of the Chinese embassy in Moscow. Deng was again sent to Moscow. The new talks lasted two weeks but achieved nothing.

Despite the failed negotiations with the Soviet Union, Deng was riding high. Virtually every important party leader came to the airport to see him off for Moscow, and Mao and Jiang Qing greeted him personally upon his return. While Mao was willing to overlook his differences with Deng for the moment, his diminished importance within the party had left him restless. Mao had no intention of allowing the CCP leadership to place him "nicely on a shelf like a Buddha," as the American writer Anna Louise Strong put it, and his determination to restore his influence would soon bring him into open conflict with Deng.

7

Capitalist Roader

Mao began to feel that Deng, Liu, and other party leaders had taken the Chinese Revolution out of his hands. Although Deng and Liu controlled the party apparatus, Mao was still enormously popular with the masses, who he had always felt were the most crucial element in the making of the revolution. Mao felt that the true communist learned from the masses, and not vice versa. Mao also still retained the support of Lin Biao, the defense minister, and the Peoples' Liberation Army. He would use the army and the masses to launch his greatest experiment in mass movement, the Great Proletarian Cultural Revolution.

Mao had several reasons for initiating the Cultural Revolution. He believed that Chinese society had lost the sense of enthusiasm and commitment that had enabled the Communists to come to power. The spirit of Yanan and the Long March was no longer present. Mao was especially concerned about China's youth, who had not undergone the type of hardship the revolutionary generation had endured and thus had not known the struggle from which Mao believed great societies were born. Mao believed that revolution in itself was good, that the tumult it created brought forth new ideas and renewed energy. Without such renewal, societies stagnated and revolutions moved backward. Old class structures reappeared, as Mao believed had happened in the

He [Deng] fought back. He made a self-criticism, as he had years before when he got into trouble in Jiangxi. It did no good. He was called the 'Number Two Capitalist Roader.' Number One was Liu Shaoqi.

—HARRISON E. SALISBURY
American historian, on
Deng during the
Cultural Revolution

Deng in 1963. His practical approach to economic development — he believed private incentive could be used to spur production — clashed with Mao's views, which emphasized collective ownership and the elimination of classes.

Soviet Union. Already Deng and Liu were trying to undo his work and were leading China down the capitalist road. Bureaucrats and party officials considered themselves a privileged class. The Cultural Revolution would revitalize Chinese society and stand as Mao's lasting achievement. By tapping the power of the masses, Mao could also act against his opponents within the party and restore himself to prominence.

In 1964 and 1965 Mao lay low, allowing Liu to run the country. It was rumored that old age had taken its toll (he was 72 in 1965), that he was under the care of physicians, that he had suffered a stroke and was unable to govern. In late 1965 he gave an interview to the renowned French man of letters André Malraux, whose greatest novel, *Man's Fate*, was about the Guomindang's betrayal of the Communists at Shanghai in 1927. Mao dropped hints to Malraux of what was to come. The problem with the Soviet Union's leaders, Mao said, was that they were unable to understand that the revolution was not complete once a communist regime was established. The revolution must be ongoing. It "isn't a victory, it is a mixing of the masses and the cadres over several generations." Revisionism, of the kind practiced by Liu and Deng, meant the death of the revolution. Mao told Malraux that "youth must be put to the test," and added, "I am alone with the masses. Waiting."

The first shot of the Cultural Revolution was fired at Wu Han, the deputy mayor of Beijing and a university professor. Wu had written a play called *Hai Jui Dismissed from Office*, which told the story of a Ming dynasty official who acted in the best interest of the people only to be rewarded by removal from office by the emperor. Some saw the play as a thinly disguised commentary on Mao's dismissal of Peng Dehuai. Mao encouraged criticism of Wu Han and his play in the press, and in March 1966 he directly condemned the author. Soon after, the mayor of Beijing, Pen Chen, was dismissed for his support of Wu. An editorial a day later in the *People's Daily* warned that "anyone who opposes Chairman Mao

> *To discuss with Deng Xiaoping as equals is more difficult than to put a ladder against heaven.*
>
> —CHEN BODA
> a leader of the Cultural Revolution, on Deng's alleged elitism

Zedong, opposes Mao Zedong's thoughts, opposes the proletariat dictatorship, opposes the correct way of Socialism, whoever that may be, however high may be the position and however old his standing, he will be struck down by the entire party and by the entire people."

In July Mao swam nine miles in the Changjiang (Yangtze) River, thereby serving notice that he was in no way too old or infirm to provide vigorous leadership. He announced the beginning of a period of class struggle. He said he wanted to "overthrow the King of Hell in order to free the little devils." The young should learn to criticize their superiors. Everything old was bad, especially the "four olds": old habits, old ideas, old customs, and old culture. He gave his "little devils" a name — the Red Guard. Mostly students, the Red Guards wore khaki and red armbands and received special military training. Lin Biao had been providing the army with bound red copies of Mao's writing — the famed "little red book." The soldiers of the People's Liberation Army still revered Mao as the champion of the revolution, and they stood ready to ensure that no one moved against the chairman. At huge rallies in Beijing Mao urged the Red Guards to "knock down the old!" In response, China's youth waved red copies of Mao's book of quotations in the air and chanted

Mao believed that China's youth had suffered by not having been exposed to the same type of experiences as had the revolutionary generation. During the Cultural Revolution, youths such as these Yanan University students were mobilized into work crews and encouraged to "knock down the old."

A 1966 rally of the Red Guards, Tienanmen Square, Beijing. The guards are waving copies of Mao's "little red book," a collection of his writings prepared by Lin Biao.

"Wan Shui! Wan Shui!" — "10,000 years to Chairman Mao!" The Red Guards attacked factories and embassies, shut down universities and schools, and held public trials and denunciations of those of whom they disapproved.

Deng called the Red Guard "babies" and was very nervous about Mao turning over so much power to them. He did not think that the Cultural Revolution should be allowed to run itself without strong direction from above. With Liu, he tried to rein in the Red Guards by organizing work teams and prohibiting violence, demonstrations, and the posting of "big character posters," the traditional way of venting protest in China. Mao tried to get Deng to dissolve the work teams, which he saw as an attempt to sabotage the Cultural Revolution.

Deng disagreed with Mao, but he knew how to give a little in his arguments in order to stay in Mao's good graces. Liu, who had once been considered Mao's chosen successor, had a more difficult time with compromise. He preferred to stick to his principles. He seldom mentioned the Cultural Revolution or Mao Zedong Thought in his speeches. Mao soon replaced Liu with Lin Biao. Lin was seen frequently with Mao in public and in 1966 stated that "Comrade Mao Zedong is the greatest Marxist-Leninist of our era."

Deng and Liu continued to live in the Forbidden City. Like Lin and Mao they appeared at public functions dressed in military garb, but it was obvious they were being pushed into the background. Soon they were forced to make public confessions of their errors. Deng, the wily survivor, cooperated. "I have not upheld the great banner of the Thoughts of Mao Zedong," he admitted.

By November 1966 Liu Shaoqi had been dubbed the "number one party person in authority taking the capitalist road," and Deng was the "number two" capitalist roader. In December criticisms of Deng began to flood the press, and the Red Guards printed special pamphlets describing his crimes against the revolution. Past sins were dredged up. The Red Guards said that Deng had misused his authority as the party's most important official in southwest China after the establishment of the People's Republic and had aspired to become the "emperor of the southwest." His support for de-Stalinization was denounced as the error of "parroting Khrushchev." The Red Guards said that Deng opposed class struggle and accused him of saying, "We should not use class struggle methods to solve internal contradictions or we would be making a mistake." Deng was also condemned for opposing the

In carrying out the Cultural Revolution, Mao relied on Defense Minister Lin Biao (left). While publicly supportive of Mao, Zhou (right) sought to restrain the excesses of the Red Guards. Lin allegedly plotted to assassinate the Chairman and was himself killed in 1971.

cult of personality around Mao and for saying "everyone is subjective to some extent, Chairman Mao included."

Red Guard accounts accused Deng of leading a bourgeois, aristocratic, corrupt life. One described him at a 15-course meal: "Deng Xiaoping sniffed at them a bit. This person had the mouth of a glutton but the hands of a lazy man. When fruits were served after the meal, he wanted the attendants to peel them or cut them into small pieces and stick toothpicks into them. The fruits must then be placed on a plate and taken to him before he would open his big mouth. . . . Because there was not enough dog meat, Deng became very angry and slapping the table with his hands, shouted, 'I've got the money!' Deng Xiaoping, shut up that big mouth of yours, that mouth of a vulgar bourgeois shopkeeper and master! Ours is a socialist country."

The purge of Liu Shaoqi was far more brutal. "Smash his dog's head" was one Red Guard cry against him. Liu was tortured and died in prison in 1969.

It is thought that Deng's life was spared because he had Mao's personal protection, but although Mao posted guards to watch over Deng, he did not shield him from public humiliation. He was paraded through the streets of Beijing in a dunce cap and forced to read aloud self-criticism at public rallies. He was beaten and possibly tortured.

Deng's family also suffered. His children, guilty by association with their father, were sent to the countryside, as were thousands of other students at the time, to be reformed by manual labor. Deng's oldest son, Pufang, was injured in a fall from a fourth-floor window. (It was alleged he was pushed during a scuffle with the Red Guards.) His spinal cord was damaged, and he was denied proper medical treatment and remains a paraplegic. Deng's younger brother Suping was unable to endure the treatment he received at the hands of the Red Guards and killed himself in the spring of 1967.

One of the chief architects of the Cultural Revolution was Jiang Qing, Mao's wife. She had a special dislike for Deng, who had bluntly said that there

Deng's oldest son, Pufang, was crippled during the Cultural Revolution while in the custody of the Red Guards. Later he headed China's Welfare Fund for the Handicapped. With him is Dr. George Hatem, an American who joined the Communists in the 1940s.

was "no trace of art" in the political operas she sponsored. Jiang Qing made certain that the campaign against Deng included his wife, Zhuo Lin. The couple was forced to move from their home in the Forbidden City to a simple house in Beijing. There they tended to a vegetable patch and raised chickens, and Deng worked in a nearby factory smoothing newly made screws. On his way to work he may have passed big character posters criticizing him. One caricature of the period depicted the Cultural Revolution as a locomotive. Deng and Liu were shown piling huge sacks of money onto the tracks in an attempt to derail it.

In 1969 Deng, Zhuo Lin, and Deng's stepmother, who had been living with them, were all sent to Jiangxi Province, where they lived in a five-room house on the grounds of an abandoned military academy. Mao had assigned guards to protect Deng and Zhuo Lin. The guards followed them everywhere and treated the couple with disdain, often requiring them to request permission before speaking to one another. Deng was given a job in a tractor factory. In his spare time he read the works of Marx and Lenin or strolled in the small courtyard of the house. Deng and Zhuo Lin were eventually able to bring their youngest daughter, Maomao, from the countryside to live with them. Maomao recalled that as she watched her father on his evening strolls she thought to herself that "his faith, his ideas and determination must have become clearer and firmer, readying him for the battles ahead."

The Chinese have a talent for finding a positive perspective even in times of adversity. According to Maomao, Deng, like other Chinese who were sent to the countryside during the Cultural Revolution,

As the Cultural Revolution progressed, Mao's wife Jiang Qing (left) — shown here with Zhou at a Red Guards' rally in Beijing — took an increasingly active role as the leader of a radical faction, the so-called Gang of Four. On several occasions Mao publicly criticized what he called her naked ambition.

felt that his days in Jiangxi helped him "comprehend the actual social conditions of the people." There were lighter moments. Neighbors dropped by to share a glass of homemade rice wine with Deng. In the evenings the family played bridge or listened to the news on the radio. In 1971 Pufang was allowed to move to Jiangxi from the welfare center near Beijing where he had been staying since his "accident."

That year major changes in China's foreign and domestic policies occurred. In July 1971 U.S. national security adviser Henry Kissinger made a secret trip to Beijing to arrange for President Richard Nixon to visit China. Mao was willing to establish diplomatic relations with the United States because Kissinger and Nixon had been pursuing a policy of détente, or a relaxation of tensions, with the Soviet Union and Mao did not want the rapprochement between those two countries to leave his own nation isolated. Nixon arrived in Beijing in February of the following year. At a magnificent banquet held in the Great Hall of the People, Zhou Enlai called for the normalization of relations between the two countries. Nixon replied, "There is no reason for us to be enemies." Their exchange marked the beginning of a new era.

Lin Biao opposed this new development and believed that China should attempt to repair its relations with the Soviet Union. Many observers assumed that Mao would anoint Lin as his successor, but Mao had always been wary of those who would presume to succeed him. He also realized that the military's increased importance as a result of its role in the Cultural Revolution gave Lin a strong power base from which to operate. He began to see

Deng learned to play bridge while a student in France in the 1920s. He played often while in exile from Beijing during the Cultural Revolution, and he is believed to be a world-class player.

Lin as a threat, criticized him publicly, and removed commanders whose loyalty was suspect. Lin felt cornered, and he decided to stage a coup. One of his coconspirators betrayed him to Mao (some sources allege that the betrayer was Lin's daughter), and Lin reportedly commandeered a jet in an attempt to escape to the Soviet Union. The official report of the Chinese government said that the plane crashed in Outer Mongolia, although that account has been disputed. Some believe that Mao had Lin and his family executed while they were still in Beijing.

The news of Lin Biao's death was not made public immediately but spread slowly throughout China. On November 5, 1971, Deng and Zhuo Lin were escorted by their guards to hear a political report. When they returned to the apartment Zhuo Lin, avoiding the gaze of the guards, silently traced out what they had learned on Maomao's hand. The four characters she wrote read "Lin Biao is dead."

Lin Biao's death was the event that heralded Deng Xiaoping's second political comeback. Zhou Enlai now became the number-two man in Beijing, but he was in bad health and pushed to have Deng reinstated as his assistant. China was reaching out tentatively toward the West, and Zhou needed an experienced diplomat to assist him. "At a certain moment they thought that I could be useful again and they took me out of the grave," recalled Deng. His rehabilitation was also facilitated by his writing a letter in which he denounced Lin's treason.

On April 12, 1973, foreign diplomats were astonished to see Deng at a banquet given for Prince Norodom Sihanouk, the former Cambodian leader who was in exile from his nation following a U.S.-supported coup that had overthrown him and led to civil war. Deng had been out of the political limelight for so long he seemed unsure of himself. He hesitated at the entrance to the Great Hall of the People, but he was escorted in by Mao Zedong's favorite niece, Wang Hairong. As he entered the hall he received thunderous welcoming applause from the Chinese officials there. The Chinese people seemed unsure how to react to Deng's reappearance. The Australian author Ross Terrill noticed how a "shock

In 1973 Deng was returned to power. His rehabilitation was made possible by Zhou Enlai, who was trying to restore order after the tumult of the Cultural Revolution and wished to make use of Deng's foreign affairs expertise.

Wang Hongwen was a factory worker from Shanghai who rose to power during the Cultural Revolution. As a member of the Gang of Four, he became Deng and Zhou's chief rival.

wave" swept through the cinema when Deng's face appeared twice in a newsreel shown before a film in Hangzhou. "On both occasions the Pacific Cinema erupts with excitement. The 'oohs' and 'ahs' are sharp and immediate. There are some loud cries of 'oh, oh.' Uncertain laughter flutters here and there." Deng Xiaoping appeared in public on over 100 other occasions during the remainder of that year.

It was not easy to interpret the exact meaning of Deng's return. Mao's health was declining, and it was difficult to predict his next move. It was not clear how Mao felt about Deng or Zhou. He certainly did not want to see either of them gain too much power. In 1973 Mao launched two new programs against the party's pragmatists. The campaigns were orchestrated by four radicals recently elected to the politburo. This radical clique — Jiang Qing, Zhang Chunqiao, Wang Hongwen, and Yao Wenyuan, dubbed by Mao the Gang of Four — saw Deng as a direct threat.

Despite their efforts, Deng's comeback continued. Zhou was dying of cancer, and as his health failed Deng took on more diplomatic duties. In April 1974 Deng led the Chinese delegation at the Sixth Special Session of the UN General Assembly, where he denounced both the Soviet Union and the United States and linked China to the third world nations of Africa, Asia, and South America, which he called "a revolutionary force propelling the wheel of world history" and the "main force combating the imperialism of the superpowers."

Later that same year Mao sent Deng and his young rival Wang Hongwen on an inspection trip around China. When they returned he asked them to tell him, based on what they had seen, what would happen to China after he died. Wang spoke first. "The whole country will certainly follow Chairman Mao's revolutionary line and unite firmly to carry the revolution to the end." This was too unctuous even for Mao, who preferred Deng's answer: "Civil war will break out, and there will be confusion throughout the country."

Mao was unpredictable, and in August 1975 he directed another political campaign against Zhou

At the Fourth National People's Congress in 1975, Deng was reinstated to major posts in the government, party, and military and was put in charge of the day-to-day work of the Central Committee. When Zhou died in January 1976, it was expected that Deng would succeed him as premier.

and Deng. The campaign was ostensibly directed against *Water Margin*, the romantic novel of the exploits of the bandit-chief Song Jiang that Deng and Mao had both read and loved so much as children. Because Song becomes a government official at the book's conclusion, Mao decided that Song was a traitor and a surrenderist. Deng, too, was vilified as a surrenderist, but the Gang of Four were leery of pressing their campaign against Deng too directly while Zhou was still alive. On January 6, 1976, Zhou summoned eight military chiefs to his bedside and urged them to protect Deng. "He has contributed much to the country," he said. "After his reinstatement he worked hard for the good of the nation. He sleeps only two or three hours a day for the sake of the country's future. His intentions are good. However, some people still cannot accept him."

Two days later Zhou died. He was 78. Richard Nixon said of him, "Only a handful of men in the 20th century will ever match Premier Zhou's impact on world history . . . none surpass him in keen intellect, philosophical breadth and the experienced wisdom which made him a great leader." The grief of the Chinese people at the death of Zhou was great, for he had been a symbol of moderation within the party. Mao did not attend Zhou's funeral, at which Deng read the eulogy. Some people said they saw Deng at three the next morning in Tiananmen Square, standing before the Heroes' Monument paying silent homage to his old friend.

8

"Seek the Truth from Facts"

Deng was expected to succeed Zhou as premier, but there were signs that this would not be the case. Mao's failure to attend Zhou's funeral was an ominous portent, and the eulogies of Zhou in the official press were surprisingly short. Memorial ceremonies for Zhou were forbidden, and the party ordered people to take off the black armbands they had donned to show mourning. Deng disappeared soon after Zhou's funeral.

Three weeks passed with no sign of Deng before the *People's Daily* spoke out against "party people in authority taking the capitalist road." The old allusion was clear. The next day the government startled the public by naming a relative unknown, Hua Guofeng, to Zhou's former position as premier. Hua was the sixth ranking vice-premier and the minister of public security. He was probably chosen by Mao because he represented a compromise between the radical faction led by Jiang Qing and the party's more moderate members.

It was obvious that a power struggle was occurring in the top level of the party. Deng was not mentioned in the press, but indirect, uncomplimentary

In 1975, he looked younger than his seventy-one years. Even in repose, his face was rugged and as resilient as a soccer ball.
—ROGER GARSIDE
British diplomat
and historian

After Zhou's death Deng again underwent a period of official disfavor in which he was the target of thinly veiled criticism from Mao and the Gang of Four. He returned to power after the death of Mao in September 1976.

A Chinese girl reads from an official statement denouncing Deng and his "class enemy" allies following riots in Tienanmen Square in April 1976 that were interpreted as being supportive of Deng. The white carnations worn by the youths are a symbol of mourning for Zhou.

references to him were made. The *People's Daily* quoted Mao as saying, "This person does not grasp class struggle and never refers to this key link. His theme is still 'white cat, black cat.' "

Each night during the spring festival of Qing Ming, at which the Chinese honor their dead, wreaths were laid at the base of the Heroes' Monument in Tiananmen Square as a tribute to Zhou. Some wreaths also bore attached banners with messages praising Deng. Guards attempted to stop the displays, and each night the wreaths were carried away. On the morning of April 5, a crowd of 100,000 people rioted in the square. The protest was directed at the Gang of Four, who were believed responsible for repressing the demonstrations of affection for Zhou.

On July 28, 1976, a gigantic earthquake leveled the city of Tangshan, killing as many as 500,000 people. It seemed an omen of even further disaster. Six weeks later, on September 9, 1976, Mao died. He was 83 years old, had suffered from Parkinson's disease for over a decade, and it was reported that he had experienced several strokes. The reaction to Zhou's death had been an open outpouring of grief, but Mao's was greeted with a stunned silence. No one knew what would come next. Both Jiang Qing and Hua Guofeng claimed to be Mao's chosen successor. Jiang Qing asserted that Hua was incompetent, but Hua insisted that Mao had told him, "With you in charge, I am at ease." The Gang of Four mobilized military units in cities under their control in preparation for a coup. With the support of the PLA commander and four top officials Hua had the Gang of Four arrested and placed in solitary confinement in different sections of Beijing.

Hua Guofeng was against reinstating Deng. Soon after the imprisonment of the Gang of Four, Deng wrote to Hua congratulating him and offering support. Hua wrote back, "You made mistakes and remain to be criticized," but he was not secure enough politically to ignore Deng's many supporters within the party. Public support of Deng was also strong. On the first anniversary of Zhou Enlai's death there were demonstrations across Beijing honoring the late premier and supporting Deng.

Deng continued to write conciliatory letters to Hua. He made his official comeback at the 10th Party Congress, held in July 1977. Because of Deng's readiness to admit his mistakes, the politburo moved to restore all of his former positions. A resolution at the same congress accused the

Students read Beijing wall posters attacking Deng in February 1976. The posters accused Deng of being personally corrupt and of deviating from orthodox communist doctrine in his proposals for economic reform. The allegations were repetitions of those first sounded during the Cultural Revolution.

A government official congratulates commune members on Hainan Island in southern China for increased agricultural production. Deng believed that the economy could be stimulated by the introduction of limited private ownership and individual incentives.

Gang of Four of "violently attacking and falsely accusing Comrade Deng." In this case, as in many others, the Gang of Four became a convenient scapegoat for responsibility that was actually more widespread.

Deng acted quickly to consolidate his power within the party. He became the first deputy premier in charge of the Four Modernizations, a program that he had helped Zhou Enlai develop. The Four Modernizations were agriculture, industry, national defense, and science and technology. In linking his name with this program, Deng stressed his association with the beloved Zhou. People who read about Deng and the Four Modernizations were reminded that Zhou had wanted Deng to be his successor.

To further enlarge his power base, Deng rehabilitated his friends who had been disgraced during the Cultural Revolution. He gave them new posts in the party. Soon two of his favorites, Hu Yaobang and Zhao Ziyang, were appointed to the politburo standing committee. Deng met more frequently with foreign visitors, who came away feeling that they had spoken with the man in charge. Although Hua retained the title of premier until 1980, by 1978 Deng had a firm grip on the government. When Deng traveled to the United States he, not Premier Hua, was China's paramount leader.

Deng's pragmatism was soon reflected in the party's policies. Two new slogans — "Seek the truth from facts" and "Practice is the sole criterion of truth" — bore his imprint and were an attack on the supremacy of Mao Zedong Thought. Deng was implying that not all truths could be determined simply by weighing them against the maxims of Mao. These slogans instructed the people to look for truth in the realities of the world, not in the catchphrases or theories of the moment.

As Deng led China out of the Cultural Revolution, he remembered his own experiences as a political outcast. Millions of Chinese had been imprisoned or vilified and had lost their jobs. Many had been sent to the countryside or forced to denounce friends or family members, and these people looked to Deng as someone who had shared their suffering. Just as Khrushchev had led the de-Stalinization of the Soviet Union, Deng yearned to clear away the myths surrounding Mao, but he was forced to proceed with caution, for if Mao was China's Stalin, the man whose ambition for power had caused him to make mistakes in carrying out the revolution, he was also China's Lenin, the man who more than any other had made the revolution. To repudiate Mao completely would be to repudiate the basis of the Chinese Communist party, so Mao could not be held solely responsible for the mistakes of the Cultural Revolution. Once again the Gang of Four became a convenient public scapegoat.

On November 20, 1980, a public trial of the Gang of Four began. Many believed that Mao was responsible for the Cultural Revolution. His defiant widow, Jiang Qing, blamed him for the party's excesses. She insisted that she had only been "his dog," but her own guilt was evident when tape recordings of torture sessions in her private chamber were played. The prosecutor concluded that although Mao was "responsible, as far as his leadership was concerned," his achievements had outweighed his mistakes.

The Cultural Revolution did great damage to the economy. The standard of living dropped, and consumer goods were difficult to find, especially in the

> *Comrade Mao Zedong himself said repeatedly that some of his own statements were wrong. He said that no one can avoid making mistakes in his work unless he does none at all.*
> —DENG XIAOPING

countryside. The only incentive to work that people had been given under Mao were political slogans urging them to work for the common, and China's, good. Deng, the pragmatist, realized they needed more than that. As he later said in an interview with *Time* magazine, they needed to be given "the power to make money." Under Deng, free markets, where farmers could sell anything they were able to produce beyond the quotas set by the state, were established in the countryside. Peasants were also encouraged to start their own businesses. The "truth" in the "fact" that initiatives increase output became clearly apparent.

Deng has been called a "capitalist roader," but it is important to remember that those doing the name-calling were on the far left of Chinese politics. The term *capitalist* is relative. Deng believes that some capitalist forms can be allowed within a socialist economy if the result strengthens the economy and raises the overall standard of living. He took the same practical approach to foreign trade. In the Chinese mind, foreign trade has long been linked with foreign imperialism, an impression reinforced by China's experience with the unequal

Deng emerged as China's leader from the power struggle that followed Mao's death. At public trials in November 1980, Mao's widow, Jiang Qing (flanked by guards), and the rest of the Gang of Four were made the scapegoats for the excesses of the Cultural Revolution.

treaties in the late 19th and early 20th centuries. Under the Communists, the country had tried to be economically self-sufficient, but Deng reopened China to the world economic market.

According to Deng, "practice is the sole criterion of truth." Only through practice and experimentation can China discover what is best for its economy. In 1979 Deng established special economic zones to lure foreign investment to China while at the same time limiting it to a specified area. Deng's attitude toward the special economic zones reflects his attitude toward innovation in general. "We hope it will succeed," he said of his experiment. "But if it fails we will draw lessons from it."

The special economic zones are typical of the apparent contradictions in today's China. The experiment is viewed with curiosity by the residents of Hong Kong, which was leased by the British for 99 years in 1898. In 1997 Hong Kong will return to the control of the Chinese, who plan to administer it as a capitalist zone and allow it to retain some political autonomy. Both parties are anxious to see if the world's first communist-directed capitalist economy will work. Deng hopes that the experiment will succeed and encourage Taiwan to peaceably reunite with the mainland.

The Chinese themselves are having difficulty with the new contradictions within their society. The sudden exposure to Western culture, the different standards of living in the special zones, and the unequal distribution of wealth brought about by Deng's reforms have led to the "red-eye disease" — envy. Not everyone agrees with the newly wealthy peasant who insists that "when the big river is full of water, the small ones will also be full." Wealth had been declared decadent in Communist China, but in the 1980s "to get rich is glorious." The Chinese actor Ying Ruocheng told *Time* that there was a "moral crisis" within Chinese culture.

Deng faced his first crisis soon after his third comeback. While enthusiastic about some of the benefits of the free market, Deng was less eager to extend artistic and intellectual freedoms. On "Democracy Wall" in Beijing the same type of posters

JANUARY 1, 1979 $1.00

TIME

MAN OF THE YEAR

Teng Hsiao-p'ing
Visions of a New China

Deng's liberal economic reforms intrigued observers in the capitalist West, but he showed less inclination toward granting increased civil liberties. Under Deng the government continued to restrict political and artistic expression.

that had demanded Deng's reinstatement now called for a thorough democratization of Chinese society. Political groups formed and published pamphlets of protest. Wei Jingsheng, a young dissident, called for a "Fifth Modernization" — democracy. Deng believed that Wei and others had gone too far, and in 1979 Wei was imprisoned with a sentence of 15 years. Today his name is a rallying cry for the students and intellectuals who feel that Deng's reforms are not thorough enough.

The Chinese have continued to press for democratic reforms. In late 1986 students rioted. The demonstrations were suppressed, and the student organizers were arrested. CCP general secretary Hu Yaobang, a longtime political ally of Deng and one of the losers in an ideological struggle within the party concerning the push for democratization, was removed from his position. Students were forced to write self-criticisms, and leading intellectuals were expelled from the party. "We fear the return of the cultural revolution," wrote Chinese students in the United States in an open letter to the Central Committee.

In November 1987, at the 13th Congress of the CCP, Deng retired from his positions on the Central Committee. He had been speaking of stepping down for months, and he urged all of China's aged leaders to make room for younger people. With him went

Deng's new policies — called by some China's second revolution — created new conflicts for the nation to resolve. This family in Turfan lives on a commune, where wealth is shared, but Deng's reforms have encouraged the belief that "to get rich is glorious."

the last of the old guard, the revolutionary generation who had been with the party since the Long
March and the victory in the civil war, but Deng's
retirement was widely interpreted as signaling the
triumph of his economic reforms, not the end of an
era. Most of those who left with him were hard-liners
who had opposed the new policies, and for the most
part the new, younger leaders supported his economic changes. Most important among them was
Zhao Ziyang, a Deng protégé who was expected to
become the new secretary general of the CCP. Further evidence of the party's support was seen in the
reluctance of its members to accept Deng's resig-
nation. Indeed, it was expected that Deng would still
exercise much authority, and he remained chairman of the Central Military Commission, which
controls China's armed forces. A party spokesman
said: "Though [Deng] has left the Party Central
Committee now, his prestige and wisdom will in-
sure him a major role in the work of both the party
and the state." He remains the "chief architect of
the overall Chinese policy." The last of China's great
revolutionary leaders, Deng continues to add new
chapters to that saga, but no one is more aware of
the vagaries of Chinese history than he. For the
moment his reforms are intact, but it is uncertain
how long they will survive him.

In November 1987 Deng of-
ficially resigned his party positions. He took into retirement with him the most
important opponents of his
new programs, and it was expected that their successors
would carry on Deng's
reforms.

Further Reading

Fairbank, John King. *The Great Chinese Revolution: 1800–1985*. New York: Harper & Row, 1986.

Garside, Roger. *Coming Alive: China After Mao*. New York: McGraw-Hill, 1981.

Hsu, Immanuel. *The Rise of Modern China*. Oxford: Oxford University Press, 1983.

Lee, Ching Hua. *Deng Xiaoping: The Marxist Road to the Forbidden City*. Princeton, NJ: The Kingston Press, 1985.

Salisbury, Harrison E. *The Long March: The Untold Story*. New York: Harper & Row, 1985.

Tsou, Tang. *The Cultural Revolution and Post-Mao Reforms: A Historical Perspective*. Chicago: The University of Chicago Press, 1986.

Chronology

Aug. 22, 1904	Deng Bin (later Deng Xiaoping) is born in Sichuan
1912	Fall of the Qing dynasty and founding of the Republic of China
May 4, 1919	Deng joins demonstrations against the Treaty of Versailles
Sept. 1920	Leaves for France to study and work
July 1, 1921	Chinese Communist party (CCP) is founded
March, 1925	Death of Sun Yat-sen; Deng becomes member of the CCP
1926	Returns to China with the warlord Feng Yuxian
Oct. 16, 1934	The Long March begins
Oct. 1936	Communists reach northern Shaanxi; the Long March ends
July 7, 1937	The Sino-Japanese War begins; Deng becomes a political commissar
Dec. 7, 1941	Japanese attack Pearl Harbor; United States enters World War II
Sept. 2, 1945	World War II ends
	Deng is elected to the Central Committee of the CCP
Oct. 1, 1949	The People's Republic of China is founded; the Nationalists flee to Taiwan
June 1950	Korean War begins
1953	First Five-Year-Plan begins
Sept. 1956	Deng is made secretary-general of the Central Committee
May 5, 1958	The Great Leap Forward begins
1961	Deng institutes rightist reforms to repair damage done by the Great Leap Forward
May 16, 1966	The Cultural Revolution begins
Feb. 1972	U.S. president Richard Nixon visits China
April 12, 1973	Deng appears at a reception for Prince Sihanouk in Beijing
April 1974	Visits the United States
Jan. 1975	Becomes vice-chairman of the CCP
Jan. 8, 1976	Zhou Enlai dies
April 7, 1976	Deng is dismissed from all his posts at the CCP
Sept. 9, 1976	Mao Zedong dies
Oct. 7, 1976	Hua Gwo Feng is appointed as the new CCP chairman
July 1977	Deng is restored to all his posts at the CCP
1978	Democracy Movement begins
Jan 28, 1979	Deng leads a delegation to the United States
1980	Deng attacks the Democracy Movement
1986	Student demonstrations for democratic reforms are suppressed.
Nov. 1987	Deng retires from Central Committee

Index

Wendy Lubetkin has worked as a researcher and reporter for *Time* and *Money* magazines. A graduate student at the Columbia University School of Journalism and the London School of Economics, she has studied the Chinese language and has worked as a reporter in Taiwan for the *Taiwan Economic News*.

Arthur M. Schlesinger, jr., taught history at Harvard for many years and is currently Albert Schweitzer Professor of the Humanities at City University of New York. He is the author of numerous highly praised works in American history and has twice been awarded the Pulitzer Prize. He served in the White House as special assistant to Presidents Kennedy and Johnson.

PICTURE CREDITS